We're Worth It!

We're Worth It!

Women and Collective Action
in the Insurance Workplace

CYNTHIA B. COSTELLO

Susana ~
may we
have many more
years of seminar
friendship.
Love, Cindy

University of Illinois Press

URBANA AND CHICAGO

This book is printed on acid-free paper.

An earlier version of chapter 2 appeared as "'WEA're Worth It!':
Work Culture and Conflict at the Wisconsin Education Association Trust" in *Feminist Studies* 11, no. 3 (Fall 1985): 497–518.
Reprinted with permission. An earlier version of chapter 4 appeared as "Home-based Clerical Employment" in *The New Era
of Home-based Work*, edited by Kathleen Christensen, © 1988
Westview Press. Reprinted with permission.

Library of Congress Cataloging-in-Publication Data

Costello, Cynthia B. (Cynthia Butler)
    We're worth it! : women and collective action in the insurance workplace /
Cynthia B. Costello.
        p.   cm.
    Includes bibliographical references.
    ISBN 0-252-01803-6
    1. Trade-unions—Insurance companies—United States—Case stud-
ies.   2. Insurance companies—United States—Employees—Case studies.   3. Women clerks—United States—Case studies.   4. Women in trade-
unions—United States—Case studies.   I. Title.
HD6515.I48C67 1991
331.4'7811368973—dc20   90–20932
                                                                            CIP

FOR

MY MOTHER

Virgina Lee Costello

AND

MY FATHER

Edgar Francis Costello

Contents

Acknowledgments
ix

1
Introduction
1

2
"WEA're Worth It!"
The Strike at the Wisconsin
Education Association Insurance Trust
16

3
"All the Top Brass Were Men"
Coercion and Conflict at the Wisconsin
Physicians Services Insurance Corporation
64

4
"Double Duty"
Work Experience and Strategies of the
Homeworkers at the Wisconsin Physicians
Services Insurance Corporation
86

Contents

5

"Like a Family"

Corporate Benevolence and Participatory
Management at the CUNA Mutual Insurance Society

109

6

Conclusion

129

Bibliography

143

Index

151

Acknowledgments

I have many people to thank for providing support throughout this project. This book began as a dissertation at the University of Wisconsin at Madison. Erik O. Wright, an exemplary thesis advisor, offered thoughtful guidance and rigorous criticism. Other faculty, colleagues, and friends—Michael Burawoy, Ivan Szelenyi, Ronald Aminzade, Samuel Cohn, Sara McLanahan, Pamela Oliver, Ann Stoller, Elizabeth Thompson, Vern Baxter, Kathleen Blee, Patricia Cooper, Cindy Aron, Roslyn Feldberg, Maurine Greenwald, Judith Gregory, Micaela di Leonardo, Heidi Gottfried, Jennifer Glass, Heidi Hartmann, Karen Sacks, Nina Shapiro-Perl, and Amy Dru Stanley—reviewed drafts of the text and offered valuable help.

The Women's Oral History Project played a central role in this research. My thanks go to Catherine Loeb, Susan McGovern, Barbara Melosh, Ruth Powers, and Joanne Whelden, who formed the Women's Oral History Project in 1979 to document the strike at the Wisconsin Education Association Insurance Trust (the Trust). The Project was fortunate to have the support of Dale Treleven and Sara Cooper at the Wisconsin Historical Society, who provided equipment for the interviews and accepted some of the tapes for their archives. Three friends deserve special recognition. Joanne Whelden's enthusiasm and friendship extended over the life of this project. My appreciation goes to my dear friend Catherine Loeb, whose encouragement helped to make this project possible. Special thanks are also due to Barbara Melosh, who, through the example of her own fine work as a historian, helped to improve this manuscript.

Acknowledgments

To the office workers at the Trust, a very heartfelt thanks is due. Their enthusiasm about the strike provided the foundation for this research. I am especially indebted to Sandra Tordoff, a strike leader, whose keen insights contributed significantly to my understanding of the strike. Judy Neumann also deserves special thanks. Her detailed chronology of management-labor relations at the Trust filled in many gaps. Susan Adams and Harold Bitters generously provided records and documents from Local 1444 of the United Food and Commercial Workers. Thanks are also due the managers from the Trust, as well as the managers and office workers from WPS and the CUNA Mutual Insurance Society, who participated in this research.

I am deeply indebted to the many friends and colleagues who read earlier drafts of this book and guided me in making revisions. Harold Benenson and Ruth Milkman offered careful and incisive criticisms. Others who read portions of the manuscript and offered valuable help include Sue Benson, Cynthia Harrison, Eileen Boris, Cynthia R. Daniels, Cynthia Fuchs Epstein, Kathleen Christensen, Patricia Gurin, Robert Merton, and Joanne Miller. Thanks are also due to the editorial board of *Feminist Studies*, which published portions of the text in article form and offered critical suggestions. At the University of Illinois Press, my editor, Carole Appel, provided support throughout.

I was fortunate to have the financial assistance of the American Association of University Women, the Business and Professional Women's Foundation, the Smithsonian Institution, Holy Cross College, and the Russell Sage Foundation. During one year of the research, contact with new colleagues at the Smithsonian Institution's National Museum of American History—David Noble, Uta Merzback, Karlene Stephens, Kay Youngflesh, Pete Daniels, Gary Kulik, and Barbara Smith—helped to broaden my understanding of technology and women's work. I am especially grateful to Marshall Robinson and Peter de Janosi for providing me with an extraordinary year as a postdoctoral fellow at the Russell Sage Foundation.

Finally, my deepest appreciation goes to Peter Caulkins, whose love and support sustained me during the ten years of this project.

1

Introduction

Working women in the last two decades have started to assert their right to increased pay, promotional opportunities, and respect on the job. The title of this book points to women's emerging sense of entitlement at work. Not surprisingly, clerical workers have been on the forefront of these developments. One out of three women in the labor force works in an office job, and 80 percent of administrative support workers are women.[1] So pervasive is the sex segregation of clerical work that in certain occupations men are almost entirely absent. For example, 99 percent of all secretaries are women.[2] As the quintessential women's occupation, clerical work has for decades been associated with poor wages, limited mobility, and low status.

In the last two decades, clerical workers and their organizations have made important gains in affirmative action, sexual harassment, and, perhaps most important, in facilitating a new-found self-respect among office workers.[3] The efforts of clerical organizations such as 9 to 5: The National Association of Working Women have helped to pave the way for clerical unionization campaigns. Notable successes have occurred in the public sector and at universities where unions have started to gain a foothold.[4]

Still, the vast majority of office workers remain unorganized. Less than 16 percent of administrative support and clerical workers work in jobs that are covered by a union or employee association.[5] And among those clericals who are unionized, the struggle to gain, maintain, and increase their workplace rights has been difficult. Employers often try to undermine office workers' unions by contesting certification elections, by refusing to settle grievances, by harassing union supporters, and by subcontracting work to nonunion employees.[6]

What conditions promote activism among women office workers and what conditions inhibit activism? What sorts of struggles have taken place and with what consequences? Insofar as these questions have been explored at all, attention has been focused on the most general level. For example, some argue that office automation and the resulting downgrading of office work is fueling clerical organizing.[7] *We're Worth It!* investigates the problem at a different level, examining the variation in work experience and collective activism among clerical workers through four case studies of different insurance work settings in Madison, Wisconsin.

The first case tells the dramatic story of a strike undertaken by a small group of unionized clerical workers against their employer, the Wisconsin Education Association Insurance Trust (the Trust), in the fall of 1979. Confronted by authoritarian and insensitive managerial policies, the clerical workers at the Trust developed a consciousness of their worth as working women. When working conditions deteriorated, the women mobilized for a strike. The particular opportunities presented by their workplace and their union fostered the development of social solidarity. The strike heightened the clerical workers' consciousness of their rights as working women, deserving of respect in the workplace and the family. It also pushed the company to introduce more equitable policies. With the improvement in working conditions, the clerical workers' motivation for collective action was diminished.

The second case traces the history of clerical activism at the Wisconsin Physicians Services Insurance Corporation (WPS), a medium-sized insurance company. Many of the same conditions that caused the strike at the Trust contributed to a successful unionization drive at WPS. Authoritarian managerial practices together with a deterioration in working conditions and a perception of management disrespect

2

for the female work force pushed the office workers to organize. Following unionization, WPS tightened its control over the female work force and recruited hundreds of nonunion, part-time workers, including clerical homeworkers, whose presence stood as a constant reminder that the union work force could be replaced. Given their vulnerability, the office workers were remarkably successful in maintaining their union. However, management intimidation led many workers to register their discontent through individual strategies—quitting and absenteeism—rather than collective ones.

The third case examines the work experience and strategies of the women hired by the Wisconsin Physicians Services Insurance Corporation (WPS) to work as clerical homeworkers. Compared to the office workers at the Trust and the in-house workforce at WPS, the homeworkers were unlikely candidates for collective action. Homeworkers applied for jobs with WPS, hoping to find an avenue for combining their wage-earning and family responsibilities. When confronted by the inflexibility of company policies and the difficulties of juggling homework and household tasks, many homeworkers became dissatisfied with their work arrangement, but the women's isolation reduced their access to union resources and made them vulnerable to management retaliation. Not surprisingly, many of the homeworkers pursued the same strategy as their unionized counterparts at WPS: They quit.

The final case investigates the impact of a human-relations managerial style on office workers at the CUNA Mutual Insurance Society (CUNA Mutual), a much larger firm than both the Trust and WPS. At this firm, corporate benevolence brought good wages, job security, and fair working conditions and resulted in a loyal work force. In partnership with management, the union helped to coordinate the interests of the two groups. When the automation and reorganization of work partially undercut these favorable working conditions, the company introduced participatory policies to increase productivity and employee satisfaction with their jobs. For their part, employees moved to democratize the union and to form the Women's Association. Although these initiatives distanced employees from management, they did not represent a serious challenge to managerial control.

Each of these four cases demonstrates the problem of collective action among working women from a different angle. At the Trust, an already unionized group of women went on strike and later found their militance diluted. At WPS, a group of women overrode extensive managerial opposition to organize a union, but subsequent anti-union management initiatives eroded office workers' ability to contest managerial policies. The WPS homeworkers overcame their isolation to forge social networks that provided a basis for articulating work-based grievances, but were unable to translate those networks into an organizing drive. And the CUNA Mutual workers democratized a preexisting company union and formed the Women's Association, but neither initiative developed into an aggressive vehicle for expanding employee access to company decision making.

The chapters that follow trace the ebb and flow of clerical activism in these four work settings. In these cases, the sources of women's work-based activism included objectionable managerial practices, structures of work organization that facilitated the development of strong ties among workers, access to resources that allowed mobilization, and a minimal threat of managerial repression. Where these conditions applied, office workers' activism was encouraged. Where some of the conditions were absent, women's activism was curtailed.

Although a limited number of work settings in one city form the basis for this study, the implications are of broader significance. Each of these work places is an insurance company, and within the office sector, insurance, banking, and real estate play a major role. Since World War II, there has been an enormous expansion in these industries that today employ more than 17 percent of administrative support and clerical workers.[8] In addition, they have been on the forefront of the changes in work organization and managerial strategies that are transforming women's work in the office.[9]

The in-house work force at all three companies was unionized, a rarity in the private sector where only 13 percent of workers belong to unions. More common are unionized clerical workers in the public sector, where 37 percent of the workers are union members.[10] An examination of unionized insurance companies can shed light on the conditions that might facilitate unionization in other private-sector firms. It also can demonstrate the obstacles involved in expanding workers' rights once a company is unionized.

In some ways Wisconsin is an unusual state with a rich history of labor activism and progressive politics. Wisconsin was the first state to introduce worker's compensation and to forbid child labor in the early twentieth century. It also enacted the first state Equal Rights Amendment in 1921.[11] Most recently, Wisconsin became the first state to introduce a law mandating equal pay for men and women in comparable jobs.[12]

One would expect that Wisconsin's progressive history would create a climate more conducive to clerical activism than exists in more conservative states. It was therefore surprising that the level of unionization among Wisconsin workers was not higher. Compared to the national unionization rate of 23.2 percent in 1980 (the year following the strike at the Trust), the unionization rate for Wisconsin workers was 25.4 percent.[13] Thus, while Wisconsin's unique history cautions us against making broad generalizations, the similarity between the unionization rates of Wisconsin workers and their counterparts in the rest of the country suggests that the conditions that promoted activism in Wisconsin could apply in other parts of the country.

I have approached women's work and activism from the viewpoint of women workers on the job. The focus on women's experience in the insurance industry points to broader themes in women's history and the sociology of work: the complexities of working women's consciousness, the impact of different working conditions on women's activism, and the importance of union resources in women's mobilization efforts.

To mobilize, working women need to develop a common

set of grievances or a collective consciousness.[14] Traditionally, scholars maintained that women's primary identification
with family undercut the development of class consciousness.
It was assumed that even where women worked for pay, they
identified with family first and paid work second. Hence, wom-
en's domestic commitments impeded the development of class
consciousness and collective mobilization.[15] Feminist scholars have challenged this perspective.[16] For example, Sarah
Eisenstein's research on turn-of-the-century working women
demonstrates that women's consciousness was shaped by
their distinct experience at work and in the family, as well as
by the dominant ideologies of the period. What resulted was
a consciousness that contained conflicting loyalties and commitments, simultaneously incorporating and challenging the
dominant ideals of womanhood for the period. Under certain
conditions, this consciousness underwrote participation in
collective actions.[17]

The consciousness of today's working women is contradictory as well. Fifty-seven percent of American women are in
the labor force, and women are expected to increase their
participation over the next several decades.[18] Many women
now plan to work in the paid labor force for most of their
adult lives, and as a result, the definition of women as "secondary wage earners" no longer fits their experience.

Moreover, the women's movement, with its ideology of
equality, has raised women's expectations for equality on the
job. At work, women often encounter low pay, inflexible managers, and limited opportunities. Women's experience on the
job contradicts their emerging identity as working women,
deserving of respect and equal opportunity in the workplace.[19] It is the disjuncture between women's expectations
and experience that is fueling women's developing consciousness of their worth as working women.

Feminism is not the only ideology that has shaped wom-
en's expectations in recent years. During the late seventies
and early eighties, an antifeminist ideology also gained a
foothold in American society. At its most extreme, this ideology elevated domesticity to a moral level and proclaimed

women working outside the home the cause of the "break-down of the family." In its more moderate form, an updated domestic ideology accepted women's movement into the labor force, but asserted their primary responsibility for the household and family.[20]

The working woman of today must therefore contend with two competing ideologies—one that asserts her "natural" responsibility for the family and the other that validates a woman's right to equality in the workplace and the family. Unionized women encounter the additional union ideology that affirms workers' rights to organize for higher wages and benefits but, at least until very recently, has eschewed issues of sexism. It is not surprising, therefore, that the consciousness of contemporary working women is often contradictory, combining a traditional outlook and a more progressive stance.[21] Whether this consciousness underwrites collective organizing depends upon the conditions women encounter at work as well as their access to union resources.

The working conditions of today's clerical workers are shaped by office automation, as well as by differing managerial styles and work settings. The joining of office computers to electronic communications systems has permitted employers to extend scientific management principles to word-processing and data-processing functions in the office workplace. Like their earlier twentieth-century counterparts, many clerical workers today are subject to output expectancies (sometimes called productivity expectancies or rate expectancies) imposed by scientific managers through time and motion studies. In addition, contemporary managers can more closely monitor their clerical workers through computer-generated records that tabulate weekly, daily, and sometimes hourly productivity scores.[22]

From C. Wright Mills onward, analysts have predicted that office automation would lead to significant activism among clerical workers. Researchers assumed that as office working conditions became more monotonous, tightly controlled, and economically exploitative, collective organizing among clerical workers would result.[23] Office automation has not led to a new surge in organizing among clerical workers, however. In part, this is because the effects of automation are not the same everywhere it is applied. Within individual workplaces the impact of office technology differs greatly, depending on structural features of the office setting. In small office settings where jobs are less specialized and subdivided, office automation can enhance the skills, leverage, and autonomy of some workers. In larger office settings where the division of labor is more refined, office automation is likely to lead to decreased autonomy and skill levels.[24] An authoritarian managerial style can exacerbate these negative repercussions if automation is accompanied by speedups and reprimands for unmet productivity quotas. A more benevolent managerial style can attenuate these effects by offering job enrichment and training programs.

Differing styles of management can have a significant impact on the working conditions of office workers. In workplaces with an authoritarian management, office workers are controlled through arbitrary and often negative practices. Management intervenes directly in the work process to reprimand, threaten, and even fire some workers. Where scientific management is used to generate production standards, negative sanctions are widespread. In addition, sexist practices are often commonplace in authoritarian workplaces where male managers convey sexist attitudes and sometimes sexually harass women workers.[25] As a naked and clearly visible system of power, an authoritarian managerial style makes transparent to workers the oppressive and sexist nature of the workplace hierarchy. Hence, this style provides a natural focus of resistance.[26]

Historically, the major alternative to authoritarian management was a human-relations management style that offered employees positive incentives—through favorable wages and benefits, as well as company activities such as sports teams and music clubs—to identify with the firm.[27] Most recently, human-relations management has taken the form of participatory management. Through joint management-labor committees—often called quality circles—managers and workers make suggestions for improving employee morale, solving production and workplace problems, stabilizing employment, and developing training and retraining programs. Although most common in the manufacturing sector, such service-sector firms as Security Pacific National Bank, Manufacturers Hanover Trust Company, Citibank, Prudential Insurance Company, and Metropolitan Life Insurance Company have experimented with quality circle programs.[28]

For the most part, the parameters of quality circle programs are carefully set. The greatest level of participation is in the employee's immediate work area, where management grants workers a degree of autonomy. Management tends to closely guard control over issues that have traditionally been viewed as its prerogative, such as investments and new technologies.[29] By excluding workers from crucial areas of decision making, participatory programs sometimes create new tensions. However, participatory management is likely to generate greater job satisfaction than authoritarian management.

While certain managerial styles provide a target for women's grievances, office workers need more than grievances to mobilize for collective action. Also necessary is a strong sense of solidarity. In some work settings, the decentralization of work poses barriers to the development of social ties: Office workers are separated across multiple buildings with some departments located in one building and other departments located in another. Other companies have established remote work centers where certain functions of the company, such as data processing, are located. Clerical homework represents the most extreme example of a decentralized work setting.

Typically, clerical homeworkers perform the same tasks as their in-house counterparts: They work as claims adjustors, word processors, or billing clerks. Whether they work at computers or not reflects the level of automation at the company. Some homeworkers use computers to perform their work while others perform their tasks manually. A few employers have established clerical homework programs to preempt unionization or undermine existing unions. With the

9

home as the work setting, the clerical homeworker is isolated from other women in similar circumstances. Hence, the development of the social ties necessary to organize is difficult.[30]

In contrast, centralized work settings can facilitate the development of the social networks necessary for collective action. The organization of work into centralized departments of claims adjustors, file clerks, typists, and billing clerks has long characterized the insurance workplace.[31] Office automation has made possible the further centralization of office work as managers have extended pooling arrangements to word processors, claims adjustors, and customer-service representatives.[32] Within departments, clerical workers perform the same standardized tasks. This standardization of activities provides an impetus for developing social networks on the job—a precondition for organizing—as women seek to relieve the monotony and stress of their jobs by communicating with each other.

At the same time, however, structural barriers to organizing exist, even in centralized work settings. Close supervision by management together with productivity pressures make clerical workers in centralized work settings feel vulnerable. In the most authoritarian workplaces, office workers fear management repression if they talk with their co-workers. As a result, the ability to make personal contact is diminished.[33]

This is why the resources and supportive ideologies of labor unions are so important.[34] In the last two decades, labor unions have started to shift their attention from the declining industrial sector to the expanding service sector where most women work. Within the labor movement, important developments have signaled an increased commitment to working women's issues. In 1973, the AFL-CIO endorsed the Equal Rights Amendment. The next year, the Coalition of Labor Union Women was founded, establishing an institutional base for women in the labor movement. Over the last decade, "women's issues" such as affirmative action, pay equity, and family leave have been taken up by many unions.[35] For clerical workers, these are welcome developments.

Still, obstacles to organizing remain. Labor unions are contradictory institutions for male and female workers alike. Unions provide leadership and resources without which workers would be unable to challenge management, but the institutionalization of bureaucratic hierarchy and procedures in unions sometimes discourages workers' activism.[36] For women, the sexual hierarchy in labor unions poses a further barrier to organizing. Sometimes sexual hierarchy takes the form of the exclusion of women from leadership positions; other times sexism takes the more subtle form of an insensitivity to women's concerns. To organize, clerical workers often must confront sexism in their labor organizations, as well as in their workplaces.[37]

This book explores the diverse social contexts of office work in the insurance industry and the different strategies of office workers on the job. Chapter 2 examines the causes and consequences of the strike mobilization at the Wisconsin Education Association Insurance Trust. Chapter 3 traces the factors that first precipitated and later blocked clerical militance for the union work force at the Wisconsin Physicians Services Insurance Corporation (WPS). Chapter 4 examines the experience and strategies of the women hired as WPS homeworkers. In Chapter 5 the consequences of a human-relations managerial style for the office workers at the CUNA Mutual Insurance Society are explored. And Chapter 6 examines the implications of these case-study analyses for women, work, and organizing in the eighties and beyond.

NOTES

1. U.S. Department of Labor, Bureau of Labor Statistics, *Employment and Earnings*, vol. 36, Jan. 1989, Table 22 (Washington, D.C.: U.S. Department of Labor, 1989).
2. Ibid.
3. See Jean Tepperman, *Not Servants, Not Machines: Office Workers Speak Out* (Boston: Beacon Press, 1976); Roberta Goldberg, *Organizing Women Office Workers: Dissatisfaction, Consciousness, and Action* (New York: Praeger, 1983); Ann Hill, "District 925: A New Union for Office Workers?" *Socialist Review* 11 (Sept.–Oct. 1981):

142–46; and David Plotke, "Interview with Karen Nussbaum: Women Clerical Workers and Trade Unionism," *Socialist Review* 10 (Jan.–Feb. 1980): 151–59.

4. See Gail Sansbury, "'Now, What's the Matter with You Girls?': Clerical Workers Organize," *Radical America* 14 (Nov.–Dec. 1980): 67–76, and Molly Ladd-Taylor, "Women Workers and the Yale Strike," *Feminist Studies* 11 (Fall 1985): 465–89.

5. U.S. Department of Labor, Bureau of Labor Statistics, *Employment and Earnings*, vol. 35, Jan. 1988, Table 60 (Washington, D.C.: U.S. Department of Labor, 1988).

6. Peter Perl, "U.S. Unions Losing Clout in Shifting Labor Market," *Washington Post*, Sept. 6, 1987.

7. See Goldberg, *Organizing Women Office Workers*, and Judith Gregory, "Technological Change in the Office Workplace and Implications for Organizing," in *Labor and Technology: Union Responses to Changing Environments*, ed. Donald Kennedy, Charles Craypo, and Mary Lehman (University Park: Pennsylvania State University Press, 1982), 83–102.

8. U.S. Department of Labor, Bureau of Labor Statistics, *Employment and Earnings*, vol. 37, Jan. 1990, Table 25 (Washington, D.C.: U.S. Department of Labor, 1990).

9. Barbara Baran, "The Technological Transformation of White-Collar Work: A Case Study of the Insurance Industry," in *Computer Chips and Paper Clips: Case Studies and Policy Perspectives, Volume II*, ed. Heidi I. Hartmann (Washington, D.C.: National Academy Press, 1987), 25–62, and Eileen Applebaum, "Technology and the Redesign of Work in the Insurance Industry," in *Women, Work, and Technology: Transformations*, ed. Barbara Drygulski Wright (Ann Arbor: University of Michigan Press, 1987), 182–201.

10. U.S. Department of Labor, Bureau of Labor Statistics, *Employment and Earnings*, vol. 37, Jan. 1990, Table 58 (Washington, D.C.: U.S. Department of Labor, 1990).

11. Cynthia Harrison, *On Account of Sex: The Politics of Women's Issues* (Berkeley: University of California Press, 1988).

12. "The Ever-present Progressive Past," *The Economist*, Nov. 28, 1987.

13. Leo Troy and Neil Sheflin, *Members, Union Sourcebook: Membership, Structure, and Finance Directory* (West Orange, N.J.: Industrial Relations Data and Information Services, 1985).

14. For examples of analyses of consciousness and women's activism, see Sara Evans, *Personal Politics: The Roots of Women's Liberation in the Civil Rights Movement and the New Left* (New York: Alfred A. Knopf, 1979); Thomas Dublin, *Women at Work: The Transformation of Work and Community in Lowell, Massachusetts, 1820–1860* (New York: Columbia University Press, 1979); and Da-

vid Wagner, "Clerical Workers: How 'Unorganizable' Are They?" *Labor Center Review* 2 (Spring–Summer 1979): 20–50.

15. Both traditional socialization theory and marxist theory have assumed that women's responsibility for the family prevents the development of a strong work identity or interest in organizing. For a critique of these perspectives, see Veronica Beechey, "Women and Production: A Critical Analysis of Some Sociological Theories of Women's Work," in *Feminism and Materialism*, ed. Annette Kuhn and Anne Marie Wolpe (London: Routledge and Kegan Paul, 1978), and Dorothy Smith, "Women and Trade Unions: The U.S. and British Experience," *Resources for Feminist Research* 10 (July 1981): 53–59.

16. For different views among feminist historians on working women's consciousness, see Leslie Woodcock Tentler, *Wage-earning Women: Industrial Work and Family Life in the United States, 1900–1930* (New York: Oxford University Press, 1979); Susan Estabrook Kennedy, *If All We Did Was to Weep at Home: A History of White Working Class Women in America* (Bloomington: Indiana University Press, 1979); Meredith Tax, *The Rising of the Women* (New York: Monthly Review Press, 1980); and Temma Kaplan, "Female Consciousness and Collective Action: The Case of Barcelona, 1910–1918," *Signs* 7 (Spring 1982): 545–66.

17. Sarah Eisenstein, *Give Us Bread but Give Us Roses* (Boston: Routledge and Kegan Paul, 1983).

18. U.S. Department of Labor, Bureau of Labor Statistics, *Employment and Earnings*, vol. 36, Jan. 1989, Table 2 (Washington, D.C.: U.S. Department of Labor, 1989).

19. See Barbara Melosh, *The Physician's Hand: Work Culture and Conflict in American Nursing* (Philadelphia: Temple University Press, 1982).

20. Linda Gordon and Allen Hunter, "Sex, Family, and the New Right: Anti-feminism as a Political Force," *Radical America* 11 (Nov.–Feb. 1977–78): 1–17.

21. For analyses of the contradictory dimensions of women's consciousness, see Pauline Hunt, *Gender and Class Consciousness* (New York: Homes and Meier, 1981); Eisenstein, *Give Us Bread;* Anna Pollert, *Girls, Wives, Factory Lives* (London: Macmillan, 1981); and Kate Purcell, "Militancy and Acquiescence among Women Workers," in *Fit Work for Women*, ed. Sandra Burman (New York: St. Martin's Press, 1979), 112–33.

22. For historical accounts of office work, see Elyce J. Rotella, *From Home to Office: U.S. Women at Work, 1870–1930* (Ann Arbor: UMI Research Press, 1981); Cindy Aron, "'To Barter Their Souls for Gold': Female Clerks in Federal Government Offices, 1862–1890," *Journal of American History* 67 (1981): 835–53; Margery Davies,

Woman's Place Is at the Typewriter: Office Work and Office Workers, 1870–1930 (Philadelphia: Temple University Press, 1982); and Rosabeth Moss Kanter, *Men and Women of the Corporation* (New York: Basic Books, 1977).

23. C. Wright Mills, in *White Collar* (New York: Oxford University Press, 1951), was the first scholar to analyze what we now call the "degradation" of white-collar work. Harry Braverman, in *Labor and Monopoly Capital* (New York: Monthly Review Press, 1974), followed with a careful analysis of the deskilling of clerical work. Subsequent research focusing on the organizational and technological dimensions of deskilling includes Davies, *Woman's Place Is at the Typewriter;* Evelyn Nakano Glenn and Roslyn L. Feldberg, "Proletarianizing Clerical Work: Technology and Organizational Control in the Office," in *Case Studies on the Labor Process*, ed. Andrew Zimbalist (New York: Monthly Review Press, 1979), 242–56; Roslyn L. Feldberg and Evelyn Nakano Glenn, "Technology and Work Degradation," in *Machina Ex Dea*, ed. Joan Rothchild (New York: Pergamon Press, 1983), 59–78; Anne Machung, "Word Processing: Forward for Business, Backward for Women," in *My Troubles Are Going to Have Trouble with Me: Everyday Trials and Triumphs of Women Workers*, ed. Karen Brodkin Sacks and Dorothy Remy (New Brunswick, N.J.: Rutgers University Press, 1984), 124–39; Mary C. Murphree, "Brave New Office: The Changing World of the Legal Secretary," in *My Troubles Are Going to Have Trouble with Me*, ed. Sacks and Remy, 140–59; Maarten de Kadt, "Insurance: A Clerical Work Factory?" in *Case Studies on the Labor Process*, ed. Zimbalist, 242–56; and Gregory, "Technological Change in the Office Workplace." For a popular exposition of the degradation of office work, see Barbara Garson, *All the Livelong Day: The Meaning and Demeaning of Routine Work* (New York: Penguin Books, 1977).

24. Valerie Carter, "Office Technology and Relations of Control in Clerical Work Organization," in *Women, Work, and Technology*, ed. Wright, 202–19.

25. For discussions of patriarchy and women's work, see Joan Acker and Donald Van Houten, "Differential Recruitment and Control: The Sex Structuring of Organizations," *Administrative Science Quarterly* 19 (1974): 152–62; Catherine A. McKinnon, *Sexual Harassment of Working Women: A Case Study of Sex Discrimination* (New Haven: Yale University Press, 1979); Barbara F. Reskin and Heidi I. Hartmann, eds., *Women's Work, Men's Work: Sex Segregation on the Job* (Washington, D.C.: National Academy Press, 1986).

26. Richard Edwards, *The Contested Terrain: The Transformation of the Workplace in the Twentieth Century* (New York: Basic Books, 1979).

27. Andrew Herman, "Conceptualizing Control: Domination and

Hegemony in the Capitalist Labor Process," *Insurgent Sociologist* 11 (Fall 1982): 7–22.

28. Charlotte Gold, *Labor-Management Committees: Confrontation, Cooptation, or Cooperation* (Ithaca: ILR Press, 1986).

29. Ibid.

30. See Cynthia B. Costello, *Home-based Employment: Implications for Working Women* (Washington, D.C.: Women's Research and Education Institute, 1987), and Kathleen Christensen, *Women and Home-based Work: The Unspoken Contract* (New York: Henry Holt, 1988).

31. See Mills, *White Collar;* Davies, *Woman's Place Is at the Typewriter;* and Braverman, *Labor and Monopoly Capital.*

32. See Glenn and Feldberg, "Proletarianizing Clerical Work."

33. Ibid.

34. For historical analyses of clerical workers and the labor movement, see Roslyn L. Feldberg, "'Union Fever': Organizing among Clerical Workers, 1900–1930," *Radical America* 14 (May–June 1980): 53–67; Sharon Hartman Strom, "'We're No Kitty Foyles': Organizing Office Workers for the Congress of Industrial Organizations, 1937–50," in *Women, Work, and Protest: A Century of U.S. Women's Labor History*, ed. Ruth Milkman (Boston: Routledge and Kegan Paul, 1985), 206–34; and Sharon Hartman Strom, "Challenging 'Woman's Place': Feminism, the Left, and Industrial Unionism in the 1930's," *Feminist Studies* 9 (Summer 1983): 359–86.

35. See Ruth Milkman, "Women Workers, Feminism, and the Labor Movement since the 1960's," in *Women, Work, and Protest*, ed. Milkman, 300–322.

36. See Karl E. Klare, "Labor Law and Liberal Political Imagination," *Socialist Review* 12 (Mar.–Apr. 1982): 45–73.

37. For critical analyses of the labor movement and women workers, see Diane Balser, *Sisterhood and Solidarity: Feminism and Labor in Modern Times* (Boston: South End Press, 1987), and Alice Kessler-Harris, "Where Are the Organized Women Workers?" in *A Heritage of Our Own*, ed. Nancy F. Cott and Elizabeth H. Pleck (New York: Simon and Schuster, 1979).

2

"WEA're Worth It!"

The Strike at the Wisconsin Education Association Insurance Trust

> We decided to tally out loud how many yeses and how
> many nos as far as the strike vote was concerned. It
> kept going yes, yes, YES! I get goosebumps just thinking
> about it now. And after it was all counted, everybody just
> cheered and hugged each other. There was a mixture of
> happiness and "I'm scared to death" in the room.
>
> —Bargaining team member, United Staff Union

In the fall of 1979, fifty-three office workers at a small Wisconsin insurance firm, the Wisconsin Education Association Insurance Trust (the Trust), initiated a strike. As an insurance firm set up by the state teachers' union, the Trust was an unusual organization. That the employees were members of the United Staff Union was also atypical. Faced with low wages, discriminatory work rules, and patronizing managerial attitudes, the unionized clerical workers at the Trust developed a consciousness of their right to working conditions that respected them as working women. In the process, the women transformed their work-based networks and their labor union into vehicles for collective organizing. When contract negotiations further polarized management and union employees, the women voted to strike.

A unique set of factors caused this strike. First, a dramatic deterioration in working conditions fueled the office workers' grievances at the Trust. Second, the union backgrounds and union membership of the women provided crucial resources for this strike mobilization. Third, the structure of work and the union provided them with opportunities to develop mutually reinforcing ties of solidarity. And fourth, the institutional ties between the Trust and the state teachers' union constrained management from implementing aggressive anti-union initiatives. It was within this context that these women were able to translate work-based grievances into collective solidarity and mobilization.

The strike consolidated the women's militance and confirmed their commitment to standing up for their rights. And for many, the strike reverberated well past its conclusion, influencing the women's feelings about their employer, other workers, their families, and themselves. At the same time, the factors that catalyzed this strike also limited its impact. Confronted by sexist and authoritarian managerial policies, the women developed a narrow interpretation of working women's rights: the right to oppose blatantly sex-discriminatory managerial practices. This constrained the women's ability to respond to the more sophisticated managerial strategies that followed the strike. The conflicts surrounding the 1979 contract negotiations were mostly absent from the 1982 negotiations, illustrating the impact of the strike on both sides.[1]

Work and Conflict at the Trust, 1970–77

The Trust was founded in 1970 by the Wisconsin Education Association Council (WEAC)—the umbrella organization for the state teachers' union—to provide insurance coverage for school-system employees. Appointed by WEAC, the members of the Trust's board of trustees were mostly former teachers. That the Trust management reported to a union-appointed board of directors prevented blatantly anti-union policies. At the same time, however, the Trust's status as the arm of a union did not protect the company from competitive pressures. Constrained to function according to insurance industry standards (otherwise WEAC would switch to a major insurance carrier), the Trust was organized according to a traditional, patriarchal hierarchy.

17

During the early seventies, the two male managers—the executive director and the deputy director—set policies and directed the work of the five female claims adjustors who performed the entire range of manual tasks: opening the mail, setting up the file for the insured, deciding on claims payment, and typing the insurance checks. In 1975, two female supervisors were hired to solve what one manager described as the "communication problems" that had surfaced between management and clerical employees: "At first, in the early years, there were only the two male managers and female employees. This created problems in terms of communication. . . . I think there is a communication problem between men and women. . . . [So we] decided to bring in female supervisors."

Management's strategy did not eliminate conflict between themselves and the clerical workers. The location of the Trust offices in the same building as the WEAC offices brought the clericals into contact with two groups of unionized employees: the professional staff of WEAC (the lawyers and contract negotiators who bargained contracts for members of the Wisconsin Education Association) and the associate staff of WEAC (the clerical support staff for the professionals). Both groups were members of the United Staff Union (the USU), the state local of the National Staff Organization, an independent union representing employees of teachers' unions.

In the summer of 1975, the professional wing of the USU initiated negotiations with the Trust management to bring the five clerical workers into the union. The institutional relationship between WEAC and the Trust constrained the latter from actively opposing the unionization initiative. Nevertheless, management revealed its reluctance to recognize the union during the first contract negotiations. One of the union negotiators recalled that "every word in the first contract had to be pulled from the Trust management."[2]

Over the next two years, the Trust grew significantly, adding new benefit plans to existing teacher contracts. Management responded to growth by hiring twenty additional employees, by expanding the managerial hierarchy, and by reorganizing the claims process. The managerial hierarchy expanded to include five levels: the executive director, the deputy director, the department managers, the supervisors, and the assistant supervisors.

During this period, management subdivided the claims process into different jobs and created separate departments for each function. A limited division of labor emerged. Previously, the adjustor had performed the entire range of tasks involved in processing a claim, but now these tasks were distributed across several jobs and departments. The women in the claims clerical positions opened the mail, sorted the claims, pulled the subscriber's file, verified that the subscriber had coverage, and sent the claim to the adjustor. The adjustor then evaluated each claim individually, determined whether the medical procedure was justified, and calculated the payment. In addition to being responsible for a group of schools, each adjustor also followed up on claims payment by telephoning and writing subscribers to confirm information reported on the claim. The adjustor's job required considerable skill. After the adjustor determined the payment, a clerk-typist typed the checks.

At the other end of the process, the billing clerk was responsible for billing schools for their health and dental coverage. Field representatives forwarded application cards from teachers to the billing clerk, who set up a file for each subscriber that included information on the type of insurance plan purchased and the number and status of dependents. In addition to billing the subscribers, the billing clerk periodically updated the files.

Each union position at the Trust corresponded to one of three skill levels: Claims clericals and clerk typists were skill level ones, billing clerks were level twos, and adjustors were level twos and threes. In the mid-seventies, the starting salary for skill level ones ranged from $2.73 to $3.61 an hour, for twos from $3.03 to $4.30 an hour, and for threes from $3.33 to $4.64 an hour.

Limited opportunities for promotion existed at the Trust. When first hired, most women worked as clericals or typists.

Management promoted some women into billing or adjusting positions that led for a few to supervisory jobs. For those denied promotions, resentment surfaced. "I applied for the adjustor position four times and was given excuses," one woman explained. "You couldn't grow there. . . . You were given the illusion of promotional opportunities and then you were stifled."

The Trust was slow to automate its work process. Prior to 1976, all of the in-house office work was performed manually: Input sheets from the accounting department were sent to a computer service bureau that keypunched the data and returned the output. In 1976, the Trust purchased a mainframe computer. With the introduction of a data-processing department, management hired two keypunch operators. After receiving code sheets from accounting, billing, and claims, the keypunch operators entered codes into keypunch machines, and the computer tabulated the number of keystrokes entered. Despite the automation, the employees were not required to process a specific number of claims per day, as was common practice at other firms.

With expansion, the Trust management moved its thirty-five to forty employees to two separate locations. The billing, accounting, and data-processing departments were housed in one building and the claims and clerical departments were housed in a second building along with the two top managers. Responsible for the allocation of tasks and the monitoring of employee performance, the department managers and supervisors had a decisive influence on the tenor of office relationships.

In one building, managers fostered a free work atmosphere, granting autonomy to union employees and encouraging casual, friendly interactions at work. Satisfaction with working conditions in these departments was greater than in the second building where claims and clerical supervisors closely monitored the work of their subordinates, discouraging even work-related conversations. Since they were located in the same building as the executive director and the deputy director, the managers in the claims and clerical departments may have felt pressured to exercise greater control over their employees than the managers in the other building.

The geographical separation between the two buildings posed a barrier to communication among the women, causing problems as the union entered its contract negotiations in the fall of 1977. The union representatives were dissatisfied with the management proposal for a reduction in leave time and a minimal raise. They also resented the attitude of the management negotiator who, as bargaining team members recalled, justified the low wage offer as "sufficient for secondary wage earners working for pin money."[3] The union team recommended that its membership reject the contract and consider a strike.

In the absence of strong interdepartmental ties and a shared assessment that working conditions were unacceptable, a consensus could not be reached. The women voted against a strike, and the union negotiators agreed to a contract in January of 1978. Nevertheless, the poor contract left the union women embittered and resentful. One manager described the union employees' reaction to the first paycheck of the new contract period: "The employees came in with their checks in April which were retroactive to October and they saw they took a beating. . . . They lost money like it was coming out their ears. [They thought,] 'This is incredible. It ain't going to happen again.'"

Working Conditions Deteriorate

Six months later, management moved the forty union employees to a new building. With the move came new discriminatory work rules that clearly demarcated the rights of managers from the rights of union employees. Management installed a time clock, then issued individual and group reprimands for tardiness of as little as one minute; directed the union employees to use the side door and the stairway, reserving the front door and the elevator for themselves; and instituted a rigid schedule requiring the women to take stag-

21

gered breaks and lunches by department. Carrels were introduced that separated the women within departments.

The changes that accompanied the move to the new building pushed the women to develop a critical consciousness
about their working conditions. The women perceived the
work rules as sexist, discriminatory, and symbolizing the establishment of two classes of employees at the Trust: male
managers and female employees. The male managers were
seen as a privileged caste who looked down on their subordinates as "uneducated." One woman complained that with
the move to the new building a status hierarchy emerged:
"Women went from having nice desks to having shelves and
dividers. They had desk buckets for their files. It was supposed to be 'the new office concept.' . . . [Management] had
plush offices. . . . It changed from being one company to
heavy distinctions between employee and management
rights." Echoed a second woman, "The attitude that there
were two classes of people started at the top and filtered
down. . . . The elevator, the fact that management had two
Christmas parties [one for themselves and one for the
women] . . . all these things added up to a sharp division between management and union."

In the claims and clerical departments, supervisory surveillance solidified the union women's grievances over the
new work rules. The move to the new building exacerbated
the already existing problems in those departments: Supervisors monitored their subordinates' phone calls, issued written reprimands for talking, and followed employees to the
bathroom. Supervisors' actions provoked comparisions with
one scene in the film *Nine to Five*, where Roz (the administrative secretary to Mr. Hart) spies on employee conversations
by hiding in a bathroom stall. She then reported any "signs
of organization" back to the boss.

In the year leading up to the strike, several incidents
heightened the women's frustration with managerial policies
and attitudes. Management refused to grant leave time to a
union steward who wanted to visit her dying father; dis-
charged a second woman for failing to call in sick, although

she had been hospitalized with mononucleosis; suspended a third woman with two children for going home in the middle of a snowstorm; and denied time off, even without pay, to a fourth woman who needed to visit her asthmatic daughter in the hospital.

These incidents struck the women as particularly ironic. To legitimate the women's low wages or limited promotional opportunities management defined their employees as secondary wage earners—as "mothers" and "wives"—but when the women requested time to fulfill their family responsibilities, management denied their requests. For many of the women, these attitudes reflected the fact "that the Trust employees were all women and upper management all men. . . . These men had no sympathy for working women and wives."

The union women came from diverse family backgrounds: 57 percent were married, 29 percent were single (without children), and 14 percent were single parents. A few of the married women whose husbands earned comfortable incomes viewed their jobs as secondary, but the majority of the married women and all of the single women—particularly the single mothers—considered their incomes essential for the support of themselves and their families. It was not that their family responsibilities were subordinated to their wage-earning responsibilities. Many of the women spent a major portion of their off-hours maintaining their households and caring for their children. For the women at the Trust, both jobs were equally important.

The Mobilization for the Strike

By imposing discriminatory work rules, intensifying supervisory monitoring, and denying leave time to women with family responsibilities, the Trust management created a common target for the union women's grievances. As preparations began for the 1979 contract negotiations, the office workers started to translate those grievances into a coherent set of strategies.

Before that time, not all the union women agreed that

23

working conditions were intolerable. In the new building, the difference in managerial styles that had previously characterized the two buildings was reproduced on the two floors. Authoritarian managerial practices contributed to pervasive dissatisfaction among the women who worked downstairs in the claims and clerical departments but more lenient supervision created greater satisfaction among the women who worked upstairs in the billing, accounting, and data-processing departments. However, their proximity increased the women's capacity to communicate grievances across departments.

A common understanding of the problems at the Trust began to emerge as the union women prepared for the 1979 contract negotiations. Union meetings became an important vehicle for developing strike strategies. Before the bargaining began, few of the women identified themselves as active union members, though a significant number did come from union backgrounds. Sixteen percent had belonged to labor unions before they came to the Trust; an additional 43 percent had experienced indirect contact with labor unions through family members. For bargaining team members, the contact with labor unions was even more significant: Six of the eight women had previously belonged to unions or had family members—either parents or husbands—who belonged to unions. Before the strike mobilization, many of the women defined unions as "male organizations" because they had never been active participants in a labor union before. "My dad had always been in a union and so was my husband," reported one woman, "but I never thought that unions were for women."

The attitudes of the male professionals in the USU reinforced the office workers' perception that unions had little to offer women. In principle, the general membership meetings of the USU were established to address the interests of the three bargaining units of the USU: the twenty-five professional staff members (the lawyers and contract negotiators who bargained teacher contracts for WEA), the twenty-five clerical support staff members for the professionals, and the fifty-three office workers employed by the Trust. In practice, the priorities of the mostly male professional staff often took precedence. This alienated the office workers, who felt that the male professionals looked down on them as "only clericals." "The professionals had a technique for talking above the union women's heads," one woman emphasized. "It gives you the impression that they know more than you do. They dominated."

Despite the male domination over the USU, the structure of the union provided the women with the opportunity to develop their own bargaining unit into a strong organization. Because the USU contained three separate bargaining units, each unit called its own meetings during contract negotiations and had control over them. In contrast to the general membership meetings, the union meetings called by Trust employees encouraged participation and contributed to Trust-wide discussions of working conditions and feelings of solidarity.

The union bargaining team provided essential leadership in the mobilization for the strike. Six of the eight union bargaining team members were claims adjustors. This was not a coincidence. Managerial treatment was particularly offensive to these skilled workers, whose jobs required the interpretation of X-rays and decision making about complex insurance claims. The bargaining team coined the motto "WEA're Worth It!" (a reference to their employer) and ordered T-shirts and buttons for all the union women to wear on bargaining days. Bargaining team members also published a newsletter, *As the Trust Turns*, a play on the soap opera *As the World Turns*. Through serious and humorous articles the newsletter transmitted information about negotiations across departments, validating the women's right to "stand up to management."

The union women requested that a female lawyer from the professional wing of the USU act as legal advisor during negotiations. As a strong feminist and union activist, this lawyer's support was crucial to reinforcing the integrity of the women's experience. "She made us believe in ourselves and feel we had a right to stand up to management," underscored one woman.

On August 1, the women on the bargaining team joined several of the professional staff from the USU to begin contract negotiations with management. From the beginning, management displayed a preference for negotiating with the male professional members rather than the women on the bargaining team. Management's behavior played a central role, as one woman stated, in "feeding the discontent of the women and helping to foster unity." Management offered a 5 percent raise, the elimination of the existing salary schedule, a reduction in leave time, and an elimination of seniority rights for layoffs. The union called for expanded fringe benefits, union input into work rules, and language clarification to facilitate the processing of grievances.

Bargaining disputes arose over many issues, including management insensitivity to the needs of working women: "[Management has] no empathy or even insight into the problems that we, as women, face when combining jobs and homemaking," the newsletter reported. "And they seem to tie in this lack of empathy with the fact that we are all 'clerical' workers. If ignorance is bliss, they are damn tranquil! Regardless of the job title—be it teacher or clerical worker—women do have distinct problems which need attention and addressing in a contract." It was unclear how the union women intended to address their "distinct problems" in the contract, but if they could gain improvements in language, they hoped that management respect and flexibility would follow.

Bargaining conflicts also erupted over the salary schedule. At the time of the 1979 contract negotiations, the starting salary for clerical workers at the Trust ranged from $3.08 an hour for a level-one position to $3.75 an hour for a level-three position. Because of a salary schedule that guaranteed union employees semi-annual raises, an office worker employed for three years in a level-one job could earn $3.95 an hour. Her counterpart in a level-three job could earn $4.95 an hour. When the management negotiators suggested the elimination of automatic salary increments, the union team was furious. "Management suggests TAKING AWAY salary increments!" reported the newsletter. "We were reminded by management [who are former teachers themselves] that we were not negotiating a teacher's contract. We do not have an identity problem. We know we're not teachers, but we're not second class citizens either!!"

As bargaining proceeded, differences emerged over the definition of a "fair wage." According to one newsletter report, the management negotiators stated, "We have to get to a point where we get a day's work for a day's pay." The newsletter retorted, "If we worked according to our pay—little would get done." The inadequacy of the Trust wages for single women was also a source of contention. "If WEAIT has such good wages, why are there no men in our bargaining unit," asked the newsletter. "Does management think it's any easier for a single woman or a single parent to provide for themselves on our present salary than it would be for a man? We know the answer to that!!!"

Union input into work rules also provoked extensive controversy at the bargaining table. The newsletter outlined the differences between management and union: "In addition to much needed (and deserved) monetary gains, we have other proposals in the area of employee rights. Management takes the position that such things should not be included, 'cluttering up the contract.' We, however, are unwavering; our concept of contract language is of equal importance to that of management." When the Trust management remained firm in its opposition to employee input into work rules, the newsletter reasserted: "Management seems reluctant to include certain employee rights as part of the contract. WE disagree. Second only to monetary gain, human rights and principles are sacred issues!!!"

The weekly newsletter broke down the isolation and encouraged the development of a collective consciousness among the women. Enthusiastically awaited by union employees, *As the Trust Turns* provided a vehicle for articulating the women's demands. The demand for respect on the job stood at the center of the women's agenda. "We will not continue being the brunt of sexist comments!" the newsletter asserted.

> Management is always on the look out for new tactics to goad we bumbling "bill senders," "bill pushers," and "account balancers" into more effectiveness and high morale. Here are our suggestions,
>
>   1. We are mature, intelligent adults—treat us that way.
>   2. We are here to do our job—not "rook" the company— treat us that way.
>   3. Don't scoff at our education credentials. Many of us have graced the halls of higher learning. But the great educator is not schooling but life. We're a smart group— treat us that way.
>   4. A little trust at the Trust will go a long way—treat us to that!

A week later, *As the Trust Turns* restated the same "demands" in stronger terms: "*We are* dedicated, conscientious, and literate workers. The success of the Trust is as consequential to us as it is to management. *So* why does management treat us like nursery school applicants??? We say: enough mish-mash."

The educational backgrounds of the women varied: All had high-school diplomas; 30 percent had some college education; and 11 percent had college degrees. Two of the women were registered nurses. Many of those without a post–secondary-school education had acquired technical skills by working in medical and dental offices; others learned such skills on the job. Management's denigration of their education and skills angered the women at the Trust.

In mid-August, management and union reached a stalemate at the bargaining table. Management negotiators refused to sit across the table from the union women, negotiating instead with the male representatives from the professional wing of the USU. "It was startling how management acted," one woman explained. "Usually the two teams sit across from each other but the Trust management wouldn't do that. They wanted to sit clear down on the other side of the table. . . . They didn't want to deal with the women. The usually problematic conditions were heightened during bargaining." In one woman's assessment, "Management had no respect for the union women [on the bargaining team], simply because they were women." Later, management denied the union request that bargaining unit employees be permitted to observe at bargaining sessions. *As the Trust Turns* responded:

> We do not view [management's] attitude as individually insulting, but rather as a group insult. We feel that the observer issue was simply a conventional ploy; actually management is not comfortable negotiating in the presence of *any* employee. It disturbs the caste system. We are getting a little wary of management's antics. Your negotiating team have [*sic*] strong feelings too. We view the right of an employee to be present during bargaining as a basic democratic right.

The article then went on to poke fun at management: "If they really are into the power bit, perhaps they should join a theatrical group. They could give a smashing performance as King John I, King George III, or with a little effort, Attila the Hun." The union filed an unfair labor practice with the National Labor Relations Board (NLRB), charging management with obstructing the bargaining process. With the stalemate in negotiations, the women began to prepare for the possibility of a strike.

As the Trust Turns became increasingly militant. The newsletter encouraged the women to overcome conventional expectations of "amicable" relationships between management and clerical workers. "Clerical workers (predominantly women), comprising at least 40% of the entire work force in this nation, have been the last and most difficult group to organize," stated one article. "Why? . . . Clerical workers usually have established some rapport with 'Mr. Nice Guy.' Your personal feelings toward management are totally irrelevant to the collective bargaining issue. Management has already termed negotiations, in their opinion, as strictly business."

As the Trust Turns promoted solidarity among the union women: "Let's hear it for us. Hurrah! Our solidarity is refreshing and overwhelming. The union's strength is built on our fellowship. We have a right to be proud of ourselves and the jobs we do. Keep up the GREAT work—group. Wear your shirts *every* Wednesday and your pins every day of the week. HURRAY FOR US!!" The newsletter also challenged the union women to stand tough over management's refusal to bargain: "VERY PUNNY? Let's talk turkey, one Turkey in particular—Trust management. That's one turkey who wants to gobble us up. *We're just too tough a bird.* We're boiling—and they're in a stew! Well, turkey, if you won't negotiate, you can STUFF IT!!"

As the contract expiration date approached, the confrontational relationship between management and union intensified. Trust management issued production quotas for the claims adjustors, warning that a failure to meet them would result in discharge, and instructed supervisors to monitor the actions of their subordinates more closely. *As the Trust Turns* reported that with this latest development, management had joined the "ranks of the Ayatollah Khomeni." Even supervisors sympathetic to the union's position were caught, as one supervisor put it, "between a rock and a hard place. You didn't have any input into policy formation. Things come down and you were supposed to administer them."

Some of the claims adjustors responded to the production quotas by slowing down their work. Management, in turn, reacted by instructing the claims managers to increase their surveillance of union employees. "It appeared that there was a work slowdown compared to work at other times," one manager recalled. "It might have been due to a slowdown or a decrease in employee morale. There was a lot of concern that union people would try to mess things up. We were supposed to watch to make sure things weren't taken out of the building."

On September 14, management and union agreed to call in a mediator. The two sides settled the unfair labor practice and agreed to let the mediator decide whether or not observers would be allowed. The newsletter spelled out the bargaining team's position on mediation:

> Next week, your bargaining team begins mediation. The mediator is there to "hammer" out a settlement; which side gains, which side loses—he doesn't care. His report card is pass or fail. He has to answer for his failure—a strike. The bargaining unit has control of that power. It all comes down to that!! Our power is in our threat to strike. We've shown our unity so far. It's terrific! We've impressed and worried Management. The word strike is foremost in their minds. They don't know how to gage [sic] our strength. A side of them believes we're all bluff and bluster. Are WE! NO!!!! If we fold up now, for years to come Management will say: "Remember 1979—They looked tough then, but when it was rough going they collapsed like a house of cards." . . . We'll get nothing if we start back peddling on our strongest asset—the threat of a strike.

In car pools on the way to work and by phone at night, the women at the Trust anticipated how a strike might affect their work and family lives. Some felt excited about the challenge of a strike. Others worried about what a picket line might require. "I had no idea what a strike would be like," one woman recalled. "I disliked the idea of a strike immensely. I didn't feel I wanted to quit though. I felt I could go along with a strike." Some felt confident that their families could accommodate a strike, but family situations provoked anxiety for others. "The anticipation of the strike made me nervous," one woman explained, "because we were expecting a baby and I was trying to get the bills out of the way."

At work, the union women developed an underground communication system. The carrels prevented supervisors from observing that women were using the phones to develop strike plans. And the women responsible for mail delivery carried news between departments. As word of management

31

recalcitrance traveled across departments, the women's determination grew. "When one woman was upset, everyone became upset," one woman emphasized. "This feeding off each other was what started the strike." A second woman recalled, "We felt we weren't going to be pushed around anymore. Management was not acting respectful toward our bargaining team. So we decided to stand up for our rights!" And in the words of a third woman: "We felt, 'we'll show you, we've taken your garbage long enough.'"

During the last week of September, the union women grew bolder still. *As the Trust Turns* prepared the women for the likelihood of a strike: "It's hard to think strike—but we must. It's scary to think strike—but we must. It's hard to rock the boat and take a risk—but we must. Our livelihoods now and for years to come depend on it. WE'LL MAKE IT TOGETHER!!!!" In full view of their supervisors, the office workers openly discussed plans for a strike. And on the Friday afternoon before the strike vote, the union women packed up and removed all of their personal and work-related materials from their carrels. This gesture communicated to management the seriousness of their intentions.

The contract was set to expire at midnight on September 30. The Trust bargaining team and its negotiators met with the management negotiators on the morning of the thirtieth. No agreement was reached. That afternoon, all fifty-three union women gathered at the Sheraton Hotel in Madison for a strike vote. The result: unanimous support for a strike if a settlement was not reached by midnight. That same evening, the management negotiators called a meeting with the male negotiators for the union team. The latter agreed to meet without the union women present to avoid additional conflict with management. The women were not informed of the decision to exclude them from the bargaining session. Management and union negotiators reached an agreement that night. By the time the news reached the women the next morning they were already on the picket line. Angered by their exclusion from the meeting the night before, the bargaining team rejected the agreement. The strike had begun.

32

Managerial and Clerical Assessments
of the Strike Vote

Managers and union employees disagreed on the cause of this strike. Male managers dismissed the controversy over the work rules as an "emotional" and "subjective" issue that diverted attention from the real cause of the strike—wages. One male manager expressed sympathy for both sides but was skeptical that the work rules precipitated the strike: "There were a lot of extraneous issues that were emotional. . . . In terms of the truth of it, I don't know how to assess it. . . . In terms of the elevator issue and the front door issue, I found it hard to believe that they were the issues that would cause a strike. . . . Strikes are usually bread and butter issues unless there is something really heinous in terms of activities."

In the assessment of a second male manager, monetary grievances catalyzed this strike: "The underlying factor was money. That was the real issue, although there were so many other factors that were presented." And a third male manager denied that managerial treatment of union employees was an issue: "When the building was built, the elevator was only for business. Management had reason to go up and down the building for business. Otherwise, the elevator wouldn't be used, although the women could use it. Also, the back door was the only entrance that made sense, given that women clocked in and if they entered the front door, they had to go all the way through the building to clock in. This was not the issue . . . wages were the key issue."

Female managers identified more closely with the perspective of the office workers. One female manager blamed the strike on the changes that accompanied the move to the new building:

Things got rocky with the move to the new building. . . . After the move, they made a bad mistake in setting up rules to preserve the building at the expense of how the employees felt. . . . Also, new furniture was purchased and women weren't consulted. . . . Before they could talk to co-workers, now they had to stand up to see if somebody was at their desk. Upper managers got upset if somebody talked. Women felt they were being treated like kids. . . . The front door undermined trust and loyalty. . . . The union wanted input. One top manager was authoritarian and paternalistic.

A second female manager concurred: "My analysis is that the women felt increasingly disrespected and this was a powerful force pushing them into the strike. It would be a powerful force for me. All you have to do is put yourself in their spot."

For the women, low wages were an important factor precipitating this strike. As workers in a sex-segregated occupation, they saw themselves as undervalued and underpaid. But their grievances over wages were closely tied to frustrations over other issues: lack of respect from management, derogatory comments, lack of recognition for skill, supervisory surveillance, and, of course, the discriminatory work rules. For the women at the Trust, the common denominator that catalyzed this strike was on-the-job sexism, what one strike leader described as "sexism in acts and attitudes."

The Strike

Carrying handmade picket signs made the night before, all the union women gathered at dawn on October 1 for a mass rally and picket duty. The administrators called off work for the day. With the target of their protest absent, the women had time to organize themselves and plan for the days ahead. Picket captains were selected and picket shifts organized; strikers volunteered to work on one of the committees—organizing, newsletter, picket captains, public relations, fund raising, or song writing.

The women were confident their strike action would bring gains. They assumed that the company would grind to a standstill without the claims adjustors, clericals, and billing clerks to perform the work. But management had prepared for the strike as well. Eliminating the steps normally taken by adjustors to validate procedures and payments, Trust management set up a fast-track system for processing claims. Although many errors were made, this system allowed management to process the bulk of insurance claims during the strike.

Unaware of management's initiatives, the union women experienced the first weeks of the strike as an exciting and empowering time, a time when new kinds of behavior were encouraged. In the first week, confrontations with management were mostly verbal. Well-liked supervisors received preferential treatment, but managers and supervisors who had harassed union women became the targets of insults and ridicule.

Freed from the constraints of the workplace hierarchy, the women found that the strike provided opportunities to assert themselves and act in new (and sometimes unexpected) ways. "When you are on the strike line," one woman emphasized, "you can be very uninhibited." Recalled a second woman: "There were women who came up with fantastic ideas. All the women got militant occasionally. From the youngest, single woman to the oldest . . . all the women got loud and rowdy, held up nasty signs, and said things they wouldn't usually say."

The women wrote songs and chants, many of which poked fun at management. One of the top-level managers challenged the union women during the first days of the strike: "You girls don't really want to be here, do you?" The women responded by writing new lyrics to the song "Copacabana":

> His name was ———, he was a meanie
> He drove a Lincoln all the time
> But never to the strike line
> He sat there so refined
> Then tried to break our line
> He's a meanie, but that's o.k.
> You wouldn't like him anyway
> At the Trust—the Insurance Trust
> Where there's no elevator rides
> If you do they'll tan your hides

We're Worth It!

> At the Trust—the Insurance Trust
> Located on the West Side
> Come along, join us with pride.

Having endured insults to their "womanhood," union women seized this opportunity to insult upper management's "manhood." "I myself said something really nasty to the top manager when he bumped me with his car," recalled one striker. "I was shocked as were the other strikers. The manager's eyes bugged out when I insulted him. But all the other strikers laughed."

For some of the women, the more aggressive aspects of the strike—the insults yelled at management, the margarine spread over managers' cars, the eggs and tomatoes thrown at managers, and the glass spread across the driveway—provoked discomfort. One woman in her late fifties described her ambivalence: "The strike was quite traumatic for many of the women. Several were not happy with picketing and did not want to picket but they did. I myself felt in very alien territory. I couldn't act as vociferously as the others." A second older woman resolved her uneasiness with the marching and screaming on the picket line by sitting off to one side in her lawn chair. She summed up her skepticism about the outcome of the strike with the comment, "It's a man's world."

For some, family circumstances were a source of tension. The USU promised strike funds of $100 a week and health benefits for the first several weeks, but many women worried about the financial costs of the strike. The single women were on their own if strike funds ran out or dismissals followed the strike. The single mothers were even more vulnerable: The strike threatened their ability to provide not only for themselves but for their children as well. One divorced mother who collected welfare to augment her minimal salary found the strike especially stressful.

The reactions of husbands had a decisive influence on married women's experience. Some reported supportive spouses who totally endorsed the strike, increasing their household and child-care contributions to help out, but the strike led to conflict in other marriages. One of the few women who left the strike after the first week attributed her decision to family pressures: "I had been raised in a management house-hold and all of a sudden things were so confusing. My husband helped me decide to leave. With a new baby, it was hard. My husband said, 'You have to leave.'"

Many women who stayed through the strike encountered "emotional pressures" at home. One woman, who had just supported her husband through a two-month strike of his own, discovered the unexpected and unsettling impact of the Trust strike on her family life:

> My husband was fed up. I lived strike twenty-four hours a day and was gone a lot at meetings. My husband did much of the child care, housework, and cooking. . . . All he wanted me to do was quit my job. It caused a lot of problems at home. The male side of him was showing a lot. He wanted to be very possessive with me. He didn't know where I was all the time. Of course, because I was doing a lot of very exciting things! And I was having a good time, but yet feel-ing guilty because I knew he was angry. I was worried about my marriage but felt I couldn't give up the strike. . . . I've never gone through anything so stressful in my life.

A second woman experienced similar tensions at home when her husband, anxious about their mortgage, told her to take a part-time job. The striker did find a job, but with picketing and bargaining responsibilities, her marriage suffered.

Some of the women asserted their right to participate in the strike. In response to her husband's demand that she quit, one woman countered, "I don't care if you like it or not. I'm in this strike and will be until the end. And there isn't much you can do about it." After another husband complained about the strike, a second woman declared: "For years, I felt I have given up for your position . . . and I resent the fact that you now put any kind of restriction on me for something I believe in so strongly. I didn't stand in your way when you moved me around the country, and damn it to hell, don't you stand in my way now."

Whatever their family situations, the strike provided an opportunity for the union women to share their personal lives and develop close ties with co-workers. On warm days, women brought their children to the picket line, an act that "management resented because it made them look bad." No longer segregated by department, the strikers formed strong friendships and commitments on the picket line. "Before we were divided into upstairs and downstairs," one woman reported. "[On strike], you got to know all sides of people. People shared their personal lives. You had to talk about something happy to distract you from the strike. You would talk about your kids and your husband." Bargaining team members were not required to picket, but one strike leader showed up every morning to boost morale. For her, "the new friendships were the best part of the strike." Another woman expressed her commitments even more strongly: "As the strike progressed, the issue became not only gaining a good contract but also protecting my friends."

The developing unity brought with it clear expectations for strike participation. Each woman was expected to do her part. Disapproval was directed at those thought to be shirking their duties. Had any woman crossed the picket line and returned to work severe sanctions would have followed. "We would have killed her!" exclaimed one striker. One of the women who left the strike near the beginning discovered the extent of her co-workers' resentment when she reapplied for her job after the strike. The union women made her so uncomfortable that she withdrew her application.

While the picket line solidified relationships among the women, management's behavior polarized the two groups. During the first few weeks, the management team refused to bargain. "They had the attitude," reported one woman, "that they would punish us bad little girls for striking." Negotiations resumed but management displayed little flexibility. To the women, management conveyed the attitude that "we were just a bunch of dumb little women who didn't know what we were doing."

The striking women faced many challenges. Since the

strike received little newspaper or television coverage, gaining support from other unions and community groups proved difficult.[4] Several labor unions—a local nurses' union (the United Professionals), a local affiliate of the American Federation of State, County, and Municipal Employees, and a teachers' union (Madison Teachers Incorporated)—did join the picket line. The union women felt that their own inexperience hindered their ability to gain additional support from the labor and women's movements.

The strikers were effective, however, in carrying off a major coup. A month into the strike, the union women discovered that WEA had invited Jane Fonda to be the keynote speaker for its yearly convention in Milwaukee. They contacted Fonda, who agreed to incorporate into her address a statement prepared by the strikers. Before 5,000 teachers, Fonda concluded her speech with this statement:

> And what if I told you that there are 53 women who work for an insurance company who, like Blacks in the days when they had to sit at the back of the buses, aren't allowed to walk in the front of the building and take an elevator to their offices. They have to come in a back door and walk up the back stairs. So little respect is given them by management that there is one supervisor assigned to every five clerical workers; that the supervisors follow them and time them even when they are in the restrooms; follow them when they are off duty to be sure that their private time is spent the way the secretaries have said it was going to be spent; that these skilled workers, some of whom have worked for a long time as clericals, get as a starting pay $3.08 an hour . . . when half of these women support families by themselves? And what if I told you that they're your employees?[5]

For the president of WEAC and the management of the Trust, Fonda's comments were both unexpected and embarrassing. But for the women at the Trust, the Fonda speech was a high point of the strike: It generated more publicity, increased support from the members of the state teachers' union, and confirmed that the strike was a legitimate action.

With the impasse in bargaining, the union women began to worry in mid-November that the strike would go on indefinitely. "Geez, we've already been out here two months and what are we talking about?" several women asked the bargaining team. "Are we going to be out here for a year?" As the strike wore on, the financial situation for some women became precarious. The weekly strike benefits of $100 had run out and it was unclear how much longer the USU would continue to provide health benefits. Several women took part-time jobs. Most of the strikers continued to picket, but periods of demoralization set in. "At times, we thought we should go back to work," one woman recalled. "People were getting on each other's backs, and towards the end we didn't feel united. It looked like management could win at times. But then, it would switch to the union side."

The bargaining team recognized that if the strike persisted into December, some of the union women might abandon the effort. They therefore recommended that the union accept the proposal offered by the president of WEAC to enter into binding arbitration-mediation with Trust management. The members agreed, and the strike ended on November 27, 1979.

The final contract embodied gains as well as losses. New language provided clearer procedures and timetables for filing grievances. Improved layoff language clarified seniority rights and directed management to train existing employees for new positions created by automation. Most important, new language required management to negotiate any new work rules relating to hours of work and working conditions with the union. For the office workers, this represented a major victory. In the future, management could not arbitrarily introduce new rules—such as the rules preventing union workers from using the front door and elevator—without first negotiating with the union.

The biggest loss in the new contract was the substitution of a new salary schedule for the previous schedule. All union employees received an annual raise of 11 percent in the 1979 contract, but the company adopted a two-tier salary schedule: The old salary schedule (which guaranteed semi-annual raises) applied to current employees but not to new ones. Whereas the old salary schedule guaranteed new employees their first raise after six months, the new system allowed management to grant part or all of the new employee's raise at any time over this first year, in effect instituting a merit system. To many union employees, management's initiative represented an attempt to pit new employees against old, as part of a larger strategy to weaken the union.

Changes in the Consciousness of the Trust Women

The process of participating in the strike led to a solidification of the women's relationships and a growth in their critical consciousness. Shared sensibilities about working women's rights, only partially formed until the collective action brought further understanding, were forged on the picket line.[6] As a result, the strikers took away from the experience a heightened consciousness of their rights in the workplace and the family.

Pride and self-confidence were expressed by many women after the strike. One woman underscored that "the strike taught me that I can be proud of myself for myself. I needn't apologize for lack of a label or because I'm 'only a housewife' or 'only a claims adjustor.'" Another insisted that she would no longer be put down "just because I'm a woman." Other women expressed great pride in their collective accomplishments during the strike. "I feel really good about myself," stated one woman. "Whenever anybody brings up anything about the strike, I feel really excited. I think, 'We really did something. WE, not I.' It could never be an 'I' or 'me.' WE, WE, it has to be everybody. Without all of them, nobody could have done anything." A second woman emphasized the satisfaction gained from successfully carrying off an "all women's action": "The biggest thing I wanted [was] to show [that management was] cold and male chauvinist . . . and also just to show the people that we were women and we can

41

do it. We didn't need men to help us. I was very proud to be part of it . . . being women and doing it on our own. And we put up a hell of a fight for so long!"

For some women, their new-found independence translated into greater assertiveness at home. Although she looked forward to spending more time with her family after the strike, one woman declared that "my husband now knows that I will not back off if I feel strongly about something." She continued:

> My husband used to say he got sick of me because I was the type, "If you can't say anything nice about anyone, don't say anything at all." And now this whole thing . . . it has been a cataclysmic personality event! Where, if he wanted a sandwich before, I might think, "I'm tired but I'd better go get it for him," now I say, "Get your own sandwich." . . . He hasn't said anything and he was very good during the strike. I just remind him this is what he wanted and he has to agree. . . . There is no returning to normal because I am a different person. I am less self-abnegating in relation to my family.

In some households, women's new independence caused conflict. "I'm a lot more assertive and have a lot more outside interests like the women's movement," reported one striker. "I'll say something when I think things aren't fair, and my husband is used to my saying nothing." A second woman found that her transformation from a "dutiful" wife into an independent woman met with resistance: "I realized after the strike that I don't have to wait on my husband because he is a man. If I'd had an experience like the strike at the beginning of my marriage, I would have made my husband see that he had to share the housework. I am now more independent from my husband. I won't wait on him or accept being put down as a woman. . . . My new independence has caused a lot of stress in my marriage. But I feel it is important to keep asserting myself."

Heightened feelings of individual self-worth were linked for many women to a new commitment to standing up for

their rights in the workplace. A number of the strike participants emphasized working women's right to challenge demeaning working conditions. One woman's statement typified their views: "Before the strike, I would have done
whatever I was told, not thinking I had the right to say otherwise. Now, I do realize that . . . if you are not getting
treated equally and fairly, you do have the right to say otherwise. . . . I learned not to be afraid. . . . [Before], I felt like I
was stepping on pins and needles all the time. . . . I learned I
didn't have to take that anymore."

The strike left some of the women with a greater consciousness of the class distinctions between management and
union workers. "I now feel that my job is just as important
as anyone else's," declared one woman. "The Trust could
probably get along without the supervisors but not without
the people who do the actual work. It's very possible that the
strike made me feel that all the jobs at the Trust are equally
important." Management's greater privileges were the focus
of a second woman's comments: "The supervisors and managers don't have to punch in and out, they receive pensions,
and don't have to pay for coffee. They come and go when they
want. They think they are better than we are. That is wrong.
Union employees are the ones who help management get
their paychecks."

The strike reinforced perceptions of managerial sexism.
"Management is always trying to make sure their employees
know their place is one step below," stated one striker. "The
problem with the male managers is they are trained in the
double standard." A second woman agreed: "Management
thinks that women are all lower class and that really hurts. I
think this is a male-female issue. They treat them this way
due to their attitudes about women." And, echoing the senti-
ments of her co-workers, a third woman underscored the
"chauvinism" of male management: "If there were more men
as union employees, it would be harder for management to
get away with things. . . . Management would not expect men
to take abuse. The management is very male chauvinistic
and has the attitude that a woman's place is in the home and

43

that if women don't like the conditions at the Trust, they should leave. I disagree. Union women have the right to have a job and reach the top also."

From opposition to the sexist behavior and attitudes of Trust management, strikers extended their experience to a greater identification with the organizing efforts of other working women. "Since the strike, I feel more supportive of . . . all-women's strike[s]," declared one woman. The strikers supported the United Professionals, a nurses' union in Madison that came close to striking soon after the Trust action. When the nurses' union decided not to strike, one Trust woman was disappointed. "I was even let down when the nurses didn't strike because I identified with the nurses' strike as a women's struggle."

For many strikers, their identification with working women's struggles translated into a new awareness of their connection to the feminist movement. Underscoring her newfound identity as a feminist, one woman stated, "I'll tell you, I never considered myself a feminist. I never gave it one thought. But not anymore." A second striker echoed, "At first, I didn't think about the Trust situation as part of the women's movement. But as the strike progressed, I realized that it was because we were women that we faced the particular problems we did. I [then] felt that the Trust struggle was part of the women's movement." A third woman also drew a connection between the Trust strike and the women's movement: "Because the working conditions experienced by the women at the Trust were specific to women in particular, the strike was part of the women's movement. The problems women experience involve sexual harassment. Most men are treated with respect. Not so with women. Women are not considered people."

Some women perceived the strike partly as a feminist action and partly as a labor action. "To some extent, the struggles at the Trust were part of the women's movement," stated one woman. "When we were on strike, we did not see the issue as a 'feminist issue.' The women did realize we were unique—that we were all women and management was basically run by men. But we did not see our strike as 'striking out against the male forces.'" However, this woman went on to point out her new consciousness about feminist issues: "I now feel very aware of women's working conditions. . . . I now identify very much with the issue of women's low pay." A second woman agreed that the feminist movement had given the strikers the nerve to take action but drew parallels between women's motivations and men's motivations for striking: "The Trust activities aren't entirely women's issues. The Trust women want good pay and working conditions just as men do. The Trust activities aren't radical. We are just a bunch of women who need a good job and good pay. I'm sure that the women's movement has given people the idea that we don't have to put up with certain things. And the strike made me pay more attention to women's issues like the ERA."

Ambivalence about the women's movement was also evident. "On most women's issues, my views have not changed," emphasized one striker. "The strike was job-oriented. It was the only way we women could get compensated. To a point, I see the struggles at the Trust as part of the women's movement. However, I see a lot of women's issues as more personal—such as abortion—and this I disagree with." This woman later defined herself as a "political conservative," but objected to politicians who think "a woman's place is in the home."

A second woman expressed support for working women's issues, but thought that the women's movement sometimes went too far: "I am a basic 'women's libber' when it comes to equal pay for equal work but I enjoy being treated like a lady. I don't want the gentlemanness and the femaleness taken away." This woman then objected to men's sexism: "I get frustrated when a woman can't walk down the street. Even my husband has the attitude that dressing a certain way is provocative. I feel I should be able to wear a skimpy top. I feel that men have a bad attitude."

The strikers were also ambivalent about the labor movement. Slightly less than half the women (45 percent) supported all labor unions and labor actions. The comments of one woman typified their views: "I am supportive of labor actions—of any strike. I supported the bus strike [by the Teamsters] in Madison. I don't think anybody would strike unless they were out to fight for what they wanted. I think that's right." Among the other 55 percent, poststrike attitudes toward unions and labor actions were mixed. Several women stated that strikes were justified only under certain circumstances. One asserted, for example, that "there are jobs where people should not strike because a lot of people would be hurt." In the current economic crisis, argued a second woman, workers should not go on strike for higher wages.

Of the women who qualified their support for the labor movement, the majority disapproved of "big labor"—of what they described as highly paid, male labor unions. Women felt that the demands of the Teamsters Union and the United Auto Workers contributed to inflation and gave "small unions like the United Staff Union a bad name." When asked if she supported the 1980 Teamsters' bus strike in Madison, one woman replied: "I wasn't opposed to the strike, but I couldn't help but compare it to our strike at the Trust. For example, when you compare wages, you can't help but conclude that the bus drivers are better paid because bus driving is a male occuption." A second woman conveyed stronger disapproval: "I felt critical of the bus strike. I was not supportive of their wage demands. I just cannot support a union on strike for a 20 percent wage increase. I would feel happy with the wages those workers have now."

Some of those who criticized "big labor" were inconsistent in their views. The office worker who argued that certain unions shouldn't strike later qualified her statement: "With the economy the way it is, the union is probably the best thing the Trust women have going for them. . . . There are a lot of people critical of unions but there are also a lot of people out of work. If they had been in a union when the business closed, they might have received some compensation." And having contrasted "good" with "bad" unions, a second woman voiced support for both the local Teamsters' strike and the national strike by the Professional Air Traffic Controllers Organization (PATCO).

For many of the women, the central characteristic distinguishing "good" from "bad" unions was the gender of their membership. Small unions representing female workers in low-wage jobs received support, while large unions representing male workers in high-wage jobs did not. Their encounters with the male domination of the professionals over the United Staff Union gave the women at the Trust direct experience with sexism in the labor movement. The distinction drawn between "male" and "female" unions reflected, in part, an extension of their own experience to a critique of sexism within the labor movement as a whole.

Poststrike Working Conditions

A strengthened friendship network and heightened sense of their rights as working women shaped the union women's response to the managerial retaliation that followed the strike. Managers removed the phones of claims adjustors, depersonalizing their work and making it more difficult to do their jobs. Managers forbade the women to talk, imposed mandatory overtime, and issued reprimands for tardiness, low productivity, and disruptive behavior. Supervisors continued to follow union employees to the bathroom and subjected them to rigidly enforced break and lunch schedules. Managers arbitrarily changed the jobs of bargaining team members and laid off one employee, while threatening to lay off more in the future. The front door and the elevator were still off limits.

Many women saw management's poststrike behavior as an attempt to reestablish its authority: "My subjective feeling was that at first, management was condescending yet benign," stated one woman. "But once they had been confronted by this small, all-woman union, they felt contempt and had the attitude, 'We'll show you who's boss.'" Strike militants were singled out for management intimidation.

"Because I was active on the bargaining team and did not shut up," explained one strike leader, "I was retaliated against." Stated a second woman: "It was evident that they wanted us to leave. They obviously thought that if they could make us unhappy enough, maybe we'd leave."

Many of the strikers wanted to quit and a few did leave immediately following the strike, but the poststrike harassment increased the solidarity of the majority who remained. "They were creating unity for us," declared one woman. "I was going to quit. I was angry. People encouraged me to stay. That kind of good will got passed along all the time and we stuck together. So I decided to stay." Echoed a second woman: "Management had to realize that the respect of these women—particularly this new-found pride—would not be stomped on." And a third woman concurred: "They tried to make us very unhappy after we came back. They did it on purpose. And this is why we did not leave. Everyone kept holding onto each other and saying, 'Hang in there, hang in there.'"

Empowered by the experience of the strike, union employees challenged management's directives. When forbidden to talk, the women talked, hummed, and whistled. Angered by management's actions, union women decided to "work to rule." "They want quality work and total respect," declared one woman. "But in return they give us low wages and humiliation. When you get low wages and humiliation, you [give] poor to mediocre work and disrespect. And that's what they're getting and that's what they're going to continue to get." A second woman echoed, "For every action, there will be a reaction. They are going to receive what they hand out." And a third woman spoke for many of her coworkers when she stated: "I thought I could come back after the strike, things would be better and I could start doing a good day's work for a decent day's pay once again. I was willing to start fresh. But, when I started getting treated the way they've treated us, I knew that I wouldn't work hard for people who didn't care about my rights."

Tensions between management and union continued into

the spring of 1980. The union filed grievances over supervisory reprimands and an unfair labor practice with the National Labor Relations Board (NLRB), charging management with discrimination against the strikers. The women saw little change in management's attitudes, particularly on the part of the executive director, who told a local newspaper reporter: "I don't understand the complaints about the employee entrance and stairs. The building was designed that way. The coffee shop and time clocks are at the side entrance. . . . I happen to believe that rank has its privileges. . . . We have to manage a business. I happen to have the training, experience, and background to be a manager. Those who do not are not managers."[7]

The president of WEAC was embarrassed by the persistence of conflict at the Trust. He therefore convened a task force to investigate the continuing problems between management and labor in the spring of 1980. The task force recommended that management implement job descriptions, staff meetings, and a "team approach" to management. It also suggested that top management more closely monitor the handling of written and oral reprimands by supervisors. Soon after the release of the report, three Trust managers were fired, many of the outstanding grievances were resolved, job openings were posted, and the union women gained access to the front door and elevator. In addition, changes were instituted in the managerial hierarchy. The most important change was a shift in responsibility for personnel from one particular male manager—the target of many of the women's prestrike grievances—to a female manager.

Shift in Managerial Strategies at the Trust

In the three years following the strike, the Trust management promoted several of the strike leaders into higher-level union positions (including unit supervisor) and first-line supervisory positions. Although these jobs carried little decision-making power, the promotions established a hierarchy among the union women. Some were jealous of their friends' new jobs; others felt that the women promoted into supervisory postions had "defected to the other side." Stated one of the strikers: "I feel very strongly about principles and one of those is you don't go from union to management. That is defection!"

If the promotion of strike leaders fragmented the women's networks, the programs initiated by management to "open up communication" with union employees defused many of their grievances. Following the recommendation of the WEAC task force, Trust management instituted a monthly luncheon for union employees to air their grievances, initiated training workshops to facilitate greater communication between management and union, and formed discussion groups for supervisors to explore more "open ways" to deal with their subordinates. One male manager underscored the importance of these initiatives: "Prior to the strike, [there was a] lack of knowledge about how to treat union employees. At all levels of management . . . , there was a need to reassess how to work in a union environment. The key is communication. . . . This was a positive consequence of the strike in terms of opening things up and becoming more aware of peoples' feelings." Some of the union women expressed cynicism about the shift in management's approach, but others concluded that management had taken their strike demands seriously.

The automation of the claims process caught the union women off-guard. The deployment of computers was not new at the Trust, but it did accelerate in the three years following the strike. Before the strike, data-entry operators used keypunch machines to enter information from the billing, accounting, and claims departments. In the clerical department, claims adjustors used Video-Display Terminals (VDTs) to access files and generate worksheets for the claims adjustors. After receiving a VDT-generated worksheet (which included relevant information on the insured), the claims adjustor determined whether the medical procedure was warranted, decided the appropriate payment, entered the payment on a code sheet, and sent the code sheet to the data-entry operator to be keypunched.

By the summer of 1982, the dental-claims department had been converted to on-line adjusting. Responsibility for adjusting the simple claims had shifted from the claims adjustors (skill level twos and threes) to the clericals (skill level ones), who typed into the terminal the name of the insured, the dental procedure code, and the charge for the service. After determining whether the charge matched the service, the computer indicated that the claim should either be paid or rejected. The more complex claims—the claims that required "human judgment"—were still manually adjusted by the claims adjustor.

For the office workers at the Trust, the effects of automation were mixed. Automation did lead to deskilling as less skilled VDT operators were substituted for the more highly skilled claims adjustors. At the conclusion of the automation process, fewer skill-level-two and three adjustors processed dental claims. However, no individual adjustor suffered a deskilling of her work since those "displaced" by the technology shifted to other positions at their same skill level—either within the department or in another department. For the claims adjustors who remained, their jobs had in one sense been "upgraded" since the women now processed only complex claims rather than a mix of simple and complex claims. However, additional pay did not accompany the greater responsibility.

From the perspective of management, the automation of the process brought several advantages. By substituting "cheaper" skill-level-one clerical positions for more expensive skill-level-two and three adjusting positions, management was able to cut costs. The shift to on-line adjusting also helped to speed up the work, as one manager explained:

> People do produce at different levels. The reason for under-production is home problems sometimes. . . . I think automation will equalize production across employees. . . . When you are dealing with an active machine which is do-

ing some of the thinking and you are waiting for an active response, you can't get distracted over paper. The machine itself—you are sitting there and you are drawn to it—it really forces you to work on something, because the person always knows that the machine is counting. It counts how many seconds since the thing came up on the screen.

The work-rule language in the union contract prevented management from imposing individualized productivity quotas (without first negotiating the issue with the union), but management claimed that even in the absence of quotas, the shift to on-line adjusting had increased productivity by 50–100 percent.

Finally, automation helped to defuse the tensions between supervisors and union employees in the claims department by shifting responsibility for monitoring employee performance from the supervisor to the "machine."[8] As one top-level manager explained, "Before when the supervisor monitored productivity, there was a lot of room for subjectivity. . . . The supervisor-employee relationship got in the way and got personalized. Now, the computer becomes the expert. It monitors keystrokes per hour, the time away from the desk, the number of hours at the machine. It is really wonderful and *the women don't quarrel with the machine!!*" (my emphasis).

The union did not contest the automation of the claims process in the dental department. According to the contract, management was within its rights in substituting lower skill-level positions for higher skill-level positions. As long as management provided computer training for bargaining-unit employees, adjustors might have to retrain but they wouldn't lose their jobs. But some individual employees expressed concern over the effects of automation: "Management is saying that the computer is doing the work and that is why the people aren't doing it anymore and why they can pay them at a lower skill level," one claims adjustor objected. "Where before you had to look up whether the person was eligible for coverage, now the computer lets you know. But the person is still taking the responsibility for the input!"

Within the bargaining unit as a whole, however, concern over automation was not widespread. The effects of the automation process were long-term and affected workers differently. Deskilling did not affect current employees in skill-level-two and three positions since the contract guaranteed another position of equal skill level. Automation of the dental-claims process did diminish opportunities for advancement among women in entry-level positions, but these women did not foresee the consequences. In short, the contradictions in the automation process impeded the development of a collective consciousness about its impact.

1982 Contract Negotiations

The 1982 contract negotiations revealed the consequences of the shifts in managerial policies at the Trust. With four of the six bargaining team members veterans from the previous contract negotiations, the women entered the bargaining process with greater experience and confidence. What was missing this time around was a militant attitude on the part of the union workers. The economic recession and the conservative political climate partially accounted for the lower level of militance among the union women in 1982. In an economic recession, workers are less likely to take actions that might jeopardize their jobs. And in the context of a corporate assault on the large labor unions, a small union like the USU would have difficulty maintaining an aggressive bargaining stance.

The turnover at the Trust in the three years following the strike provided an additional reason for the reduced militance. Fifteen to twenty new employees were hired to replace the women who quit. Strikers did make efforts to educate the newcomers about the strike. Not having shared the experience of the strike, many of the new employees were reluctant to involve themselves in union activities. For long-term employees, intimate knowledge of the costs of a strike contributed to a cautious attitude. Although they reaffirmed their commitment to "take action in the face of harassment," the veterans of the 1979 action also saw a strike as a strategy of last resort.

Most important, the shifts in managerial policies at the Trust removed the basis for the acute and pervasive dissatisfactions that had catalyzed the strike. In 1979, the explicit forms of management harassment and discrimination provided a common, personalized target for the women's grievances. In contrast, management's poststrike strategies did not provoke this same type of dissatisfaction. As one office worker put it, "The feeling is we won't have to strike. The mental and emotional cruelty isn't there."

The bargaining team entered negotiations with a proposal that protected union input into work rules, extended union benefits, increased union wages, and introduced flextime. Management proposed a minimal salary increase and production standards, as well as a reduction in leave time. Once again, the bargaining team started a newsletter, *On the Front*. The newsletter reported that initially the atmosphere at bargaining was "cooperative" and "congenial" but midway through the process, echoes of the prestrike militance surfaced when the management bargaining team proved inflexible on salaries: "Sunday's session indicates that the Employer has confused our amiability with ignorance and this does offend us. We really do possess capability beyond that of whipping up a batch of chocolate chip cookies and determining which end of the baby to diaper. We have been around this dance floor once or twice and, ladies, it does take two to tango, but we don't think the Employer has reached the waltz tempo yet!"

In November of 1982, union and management reached agreement on the contract. The union retained its leave time and gained a moderate raise (of 4.5 percent the first year, 7.5 percent the second year, and 8 percent the third year), but lost language on work rules. Whereas the language in the 1979 contract required management to bargain any new work rules with the union, the new language made work rules subject to union grievance after their implementation.

Union women were unhappy with the 1982 contract, particularly with the loss of control over work rules. "To go from language saying the union has to agree on work rules to that they have to talk to the union and then the union can arbitrate is like going from a Rolls Royce to a bicycle," declared one strike leader. "Ultimately, management could implement work rules around production standards.... That would kill us.... With the previous language, management couldn't have done this."

Grievances also surfaced over the inequities in the salary schedule. In preparing for the 1982 negotiations, the union discovered that the final 1979 contract had omitted some important language regarding the salary schedule. The union women had interpreted the mediator-arbitrator's award to require management to bring employees up to their maximum salary level within a specified period of time. This language was absent, however, from the final contract. The union filed a grievance over this issue before the 1979 contract expired. The women would have to wait almost three years before receiving a final ruling on this grievance.

Epilogue

In the spring of 1985, an arbitrator sided with management on the grievance over the salary schedule: Management was not required to award back pay to its employees. The company did agree, however, to review the cases of those employees whose pay fell significantly below the levels they would have received had the original language been included in the contract. As a result, approximately thirty employees received raises, and many of the office workers interpreted this action as a good-faith effort on management's part.

Six years after the strike, improvements in working conditions were evident at the Trust. A new executive director was hired who encouraged management to work cooperatively with union employees. Office workers expressed guarded optimism regarding the impact of the change at the top on management-union relations. At least in the short run, management had not taken advantage of the 1982 change in the language over work rules. Productivity standards had not been introduced. Supervisors received weekly printouts on productivity and error rates but did not use them to impose individualized productivity expectancies on union employees. Automation was proceeding slowly, with mixed consequences for different groups of office workers. In the dental-claims department, there were now two skilled adjustors where six had worked in 1979. Several new skilled positions had been added to the department, partially offsetting the downgrading of the adjusting process. In the health-claims department, sixteen health adjustors continued to process claims manually, although plans were underway to automate the process.

Office workers at the Trust expressed mixed views about their working conditions. A survey conducted in July of 1985 by the University of Wisconsin concluded that job satisfaction was higher among clerical workers at the Trust compared to regional norms for bargaining unit employees.[9] But the survey also found that dissatisfaction persisted with company policies and practices, physical working conditions, and promotional opportunities. In particular, union employees felt that positive feedback was rare and the tone of management memos was often condescending. Those hired before May 1981 expressed lower levels of satisfaction than those hired more recently, perhaps reflecting the persistence of critical attitudes among strike participants.

Strike leaders agreed that working conditions had improved significantly since 1979, but residual problems remained, particularly in managerial attitudes, productivity pressures, and pay. For one woman, the persistence of class distinctions between management and union was the issue. That supervisors didn't have to punch in, received a better retirement plan, and "acted superior" provoked frustration:

> I think we would be a much happier group if they would really cut out the two classes. Sometimes, I feel there is a certain mentality in certain areas where they still want you to know that they are superior beings and they are not. We are all equal. They make more money and have a better job

56

than I do but we are equal. . . . Whenever I get depressed or irritated, that is the thing that really irritates me. It really bugs me. . . . I want to be treated like a professional, someone who can come to work and not have to punch a time clock.

For a second woman, the productivity pressures—in her estimation a precursor of what was to come with automation in the health-claims department—were unfair: "They've been really push, push, pushing to get the production. . . . You know, it's push it out, push it out. And I know that the data [that they are collecting] is what they are going to base their production standards on. . . . I'm not a computer, you can't pull out my floppy disk. . . . I'm not the only one feeling those frustrations. There is a lot of pressure. Things are changing so quickly, today you do it this way and tomorrow another way." And for a third strike leader, the central problem boiled down to the low wages and value placed on office work:

I think that women in this kind of industry do not make the kind of money that we should. I still believe that for office workers, the salaries are lower than for different jobs that men have. I still would like to see that somehow the whole industry of what we do in our jobs is valued more than what it is now. I still do not think that our jobs have a lot of value to them. We value them and we know what we do personally. But the overall picture is, "Oh she is a clerical worker" . . . the old clerical worker routine. I still would like to see the whole industry be upgraded.

No doubt, the views of strike leaders were more critical than the views of many of their co-workers at the Trust, reflecting a consciousness born of the strike experience. This consciousness continued to shape the women's assessment of working conditions and separated the strikers from those hired later. Among the strikers, a "quiet sisterhood" persisted. So powerful was the strike experience for some women that even six years later, when one striker began a sentence, another "seventy-niner" would often finish it for her. But for women hired after the strike, the experience seemed distant and unfamiliar. Friendships formed across the two groups, but the type of bonds forged during the strike did not. As one striker described it:

> I think that most of the people who went on strike, wherever they are, whether they are management or union, they are still close. With the new people, it's a different story. We still talk about stories and the strike and say, "Remember when we did this and that . . ." and the new people just kind of look at us and say, "So what, this happened so many years ago, we don't really care if we hear this stuff." I don't think we have half of the solidarity that we had when we went on strike in terms of the whole group. I don't really think we do. But for the people who went on strike, we still have that bond.

Conclusion

The strike at the Trust offers powerful testimony to the capacity of office workers to respond to authoritarian and patriarchal management policies with militant collective action. Confronted with discriminatory practices and attitudes as well as a hierarchy of surveillance and control, these women initiated a strike. For many of the women, the strike provoked ambivalence. It required that they risk financial hardship, challenge traditional power relationships with management and husbands, and confront conventional expectations about proper feminine behavior. For all but a few of the women, misgivings were overridden by a commitment to "see the strike through." Still, the working conditions at the Trust were not unusual. Although the Trust management's institutionalization of discriminatory work rules was particularly shortsighted, an authoritarian managerial style is not uncommon in the insurance industry. Collective actions, however, are rare. At the Trust, a unique set of circumstances encouraged these office workers to translate grievances into a strike mobilization.

First, the structure of work at this company facilitated communication among the office workers. With the centralization of all the departments in one building, the proximity of office workers encouraged the identification of a common understanding about working conditions. Second, union resources were a crucial factor in this strike mobilization. Although none of the women had participated in a strike before, previous contact with trade unions legitimated labor actions for many of them. In addition, the division of the USU into three bargaining units allowed the Trust women to shape their own unit to reflect their needs and interests. Although the women were forced to confront sexism in their union as well as their workplace, the moral encouragement and legal advice from key professional members of the union provided an important resource for this action. Finally, the institutional relationship between the Trust and WEAC diminished the threat of management repression. Concerned with its image as a labor organization, WEAC constrained the Trust from mobilizing for aggressive anti-union initiatives. Unlike other insurance companies, the Trust was unable to threaten the union employees with nonunion replacements should they go on strike.

In one sense, the Trust strike resembles strikes among male workers: When grievances accumulated to the bursting point, these clerical workers went on strike. But in another sense, this strike also underscores the centrality of gender in shaping women's work-based activism. The working conditions at this company were defined by both class and gender hierarchies. Not only were the office workers paid low wages for clerical jobs that granted them little autonomy, negligible authority, and minimal promotional opportunities but the managers who set the policies were men. Many of management's practices were shaped by sexist assumptions regarding women's status as "secondary wage earners." Other policies, such as the work rules imposed by management with the move to the new building, are not unusual in workplaces employing mostly male workers, but because these rules were instituted by male managers whose policies reflected patriarchal attitudes, the women defined the work rules as sexist.

Gender also shaped the emerging consciousness of the Trust women. Like other working women, the office workers brought into the workplace a gender identification based on their dual responsibilities as wage earners and family members. These office workers saw themselves not as workers or women, but as working women, simultaneously responsible for earning an income and maintaining a household. Contrary to management's view, the women took pride in their responsibilities in both spheres. It was against this backdrop that these office workers developed a female-centered consciousness regarding working conditions at the Trust. At the core of this consiousness was the perception that management's actions were patronizing, sexist, and disrespectful of their status as working women.

In addition, gender shaped the emergence of a militant work culture. As these office workers began to organize, they incorporated traditional women's rituals into their work culture. Nowhere was this more obvious than in naming their newsletter *As the Trust Turns*. More than a reflection of traditional women's values, the newsletter used women's commitments to family to urge its readers to develop a sense of entitlement at work.

Once on strike, the culture of these office workers became more radical still. Openly and vocally challenging the right of male managers to assume the power of their position, the Trust women became increasingly militant. From opposition to the patriarchal behavior and attitudes of management, many of the women concluded the strike with a heightened appreciation of feminist issues and the working women's movement. And for many women the strike encouraged their assertion of greater equality in the home.

What can this strike tell us about the possibilities as well as the limitations of collective actions forged around the theme of working women's rights? On the one hand, the Trust women went beyond the narrow demands of workers for wages and benefits to demand that negotiations between management and union women be dictated by "human rights and principles." For the women at the Trust, this meant respect for their status as working women, equal treatment in regard to work rules, and a heightened sensitivity to the particular responsibilities and problems women bring to and encounter on the job. In the context of working conditions at this company, these were radical demands necessitating radical action.

But on the other hand, as dramatic as this strike was, it would be a mistake to misinterpret the lessons these women took away from their experience. Like other participants in collective action, these office workers incorporated the lessons of the strike into preexisting ideas about work and family. Prior to this action, traditional values about women's roles coexisted with a latent sense of women's rights in the workplace. Based on their encounters with managerial sexism and harassment, the union women developed a particular interpretation of working women's rights: the right to oppose blatantly discriminatory management practices and to demand respectful treatment on the job and in the family.

Even the demand for strong union input into work rules— a radical demand in any management-labor dispute—was motivated by particular objections to discriminatory work rules, not by more general grievances over union exclusion from managerial decision making. For most of the women, their consciousness of work-based rights did not extend to their right to control other aspects of their working conditions. As a result, management's poststrike strategies caught the women off-guard.

The promotions of strike leaders were controversial, but women directed their resentment toward their co-workers rather than management. The institution of a more participatory approach led to cynicism among some women, but it generated acceptance of their working conditions among others. And the automation of the claims process caused concern, but most women did not perceive the potential hazards in office automation.

We're Worth It!

Though the shift in managerial styles that followed the strike defused the women's militance, other factors were also important. The turnover among office workers fragmented the solidarity that had emerged during the strike, and the recession of the early eighties, together with the continued weakening of the labor movement as a whole, discouraged women's activism. But the primary factor responsible for the changed tenor of management-labor relations was the improvement in working conditions in the years following the strike. In the absence of pervasive dissatisfaction among office workers, acute conflict gave way to greater cooperation at the Trust.

NOTES

1. The data for chapter 2 were derived from twenty-two in-depth semistructured interviews and thirty-seven short written interviews with office workers at the Trust, together with six semistructured interviews with Trust managers and an interview with the lawyer who provided legal support for the 1979 contract negotiations. The oral interviews with office workers covered work and family history, union background, work and family attitudes, working conditions at the Trust, the strike, and poststrike working conditions. The short written interviews included demographic questions as well as questions on work and family history, union background, and extent of strike participation. The interviews with Trust managers included questions on managerial policies, decisions, and attitudes regarding the organization of work and the strike. The interviews have been slightly edited for grammar and punctuation. Additional materials for this chapter—union newsletters, grievances, and labor contracts—were provided by the union.

2. Document provided by Judy Neumann, legal advisor to the Trust women for the 1979 negotiations and lawyer for the WEAC.

3. It is difficult to assess objectively what Trust managers actually said. Throughout the interviews, the union women referred to comments and attitudes of the male managers they found particularly offensive. The determination of the accuracy of managerial statements is less important than the shared understandings of the women about those statements.

4. Two years before the Trust strike, a bitter strike had taken place at the major Madison newspapers owned by Madison Newspaper, Inc. This may partially explain the low level of newspaper

women's strike may also have been a factor.

5. Jane Fonda speech, WEA Convention, Oct. 25, 1979. Document
provided by the United Staff Union.

6. See Temma Kaplan, "Female Consciousness and Collective Action: The Case of Barcelona, 1910–1918," *Signs* 7 (Spring 1982): 545–66.

7. Crista Zivanovic, "Office Women See Working Conditions as Blatant Sexism," *Capitol Times*, Apr. 7, 1980.

8. For an analysis of management's use of technology to displace conflict, see David Noble, "Social Choice in Machine Design: The Case of Automatically Controlled Machine Tools," in *Case Studies on the Labor Process*, ed. Andrew Zimbalist (New York: Monthly Review Press, 1979), 18–50.

9. Center for the Study of Organizational Productivity, Graduate School of Business, University of Wisconsin, "WEA Insurance Trust: Organizational Survey, Feedback Report," July 10, 1985.

3

"All the Top Brass Were Men"

Coercion and Conflict at the Wisconsin Physicians Services Insurance Corporation

> [The President of WPS] is the general and everyone else is a private. . . . Anybody who threatens his power is gotten rid of in one way or another. [Management] treats all the women like they are in the military but eventually this mistreatment will come back to haunt them.
>
> —Office worker, Wisconsin Physicians
> Services Insurance Corporation

Across town from the Trust a second group of office workers confronted equally problematic conditions at the Wisconsin Physicians Services Insurance Corporation (WPS). When working conditions at this medium-sized insurance company took a turn for the worse in the midseventies, the employees voted to affiliate with a labor union. The company responded by harassing union supporters and instituting a rigid and authoritarian set of policies throughout the firm. Conflict between management and union employees at WPS peaked in 1979 when the union threatened a strike but later backed off after the company offered a union shop. Subsequently, management's decision to hire hundreds of nonunion, part-time office workers—including more than one hundred clerical homeworkers—weakened the office workers' capacity to challenge the company.

The unionization drive at WPS was sparked by many of the same factors that catalyzed the strike at the Trust. A move to a new building brought with it a deterioration in working conditions that crystallized the office workers' grievances while opportunities to communicate shared grievances increased. The two companies differed in one important respect, however. The ties between the Trust and a labor union constrained Trust management during the strike and led to improvements following the strike. WPS management faced no comparable institutional pressures and, if anything, conditions worsened following unionization. Continued harassment provoked employee dissatisfaction but it also created a climate of fear that impeded clerical activism.[1]

Work and Conflict at WPS

WPS was founded in 1946 by the State Medical Society (SMS), a professional association of Wisconsin doctors. In the midseventies, approximately four hundred office workers processed health claims at WPS. Like the Trust, WPS responded to growth by expanding to several office buildings, by streamlining the work process, and by introducing computers. The larger size of WPS allowed for greater specialization of the claims process. An entire floor of one building, for example, was devoted to processing Medicare claims.

Despite its greater size, WPS was only slightly more automated than the Trust by the midseventies. The Medicare department used Video-Display Terminals for on-line adjusting, but many departments processed claims through a combination of manual and keypunch systems: After confirming the fee for service, claims adjustors coded the appropriate information on code sheets and keypunch operators entered the coded information into the computer. WPS had not automated more of its work process because adjustors specializing in the processing of one type of claim could achieve great speed in a short period of time. As a manager explained, "People were almost as fast as the computer."

WPS was an authoritarian company. The president maintained a tight monopoly of control over all policies, employing a small cadre of loyal managers to carry out his directives. "The president had the attitude," explained one manager, "that you will do this and I am deciding as the president what the priorities will be." Excluded from input into company policies, some middle managers were uneasy with the arrangement. "We were told to get subordinates to do things or else," stated one manager. "Managers were dissatisfied with the decision-making process and how we were instructed to treat our subordinates. It was difficult to get loyalty and have humanitarian arrangements."

Arbitrary decisions were commonplace at WPS. Management granted new employees higher wages than long-term employees performing the same job and decided on promotions and raises arbitrarily. "It was all in who you knew," emphasized one office worker. Some long-term office workers had never received a raise or promotion. Others found that a promotion did not necessarily bring a raise since the company sometimes downgraded the new position to the salary level associated with the old one. Management was unsympathetic to employee objections to these practices.

In 1974, several developments heightened employee dissatisfaction with working conditions at WPS. The state insurance commissioner filed an antitrust suit against WPS, charging that the institutional relationship between the company and the SMS represented a conflict of interest (because SMS doctors could influence insurance rates to their advantage). The impending separation of WPS from SMS threatened the employees' insurance benefits—the one compensation for the low wages and negligible promotional opportunities at WPS.

Then, WPS moved all its employees to a new building. The top executives received plush new offices, but small cubicles awaited the office workers. "[The top managers] had gold-plated faucets and knee-deep carpets," recalled one woman. "[It] looked like a set from a movie. [I thought,] why do you have to show us this. . . . Do you want us to feel worse than we already do?" For WPS employees, the contrast between management's extravagant offices and the "sweatshop conditions" of the clerical staff symbolized the gender hierarchy at the company. Declared one office worker, "At WPS, all the top brass were men and they had the power."

The move to the new building brought with it productivity standards and layoffs. The company hired consultants to streamline the claims adjustors' work. As a result, management eliminated some jobs and announced that layoffs would follow. "Lots of women ended up crying in the bathroom," reported one woman. "It was a bad decision on the part of the company. The company should have consulted the employees about improvements in efficiency. They treated the employees like they were a notch below intelligent. It was grossly unfair." For those employees who remained, the productivity expectancies, or "reasonable expectancies" (REs) as they were called at WPS, became the basis for more rigid and standardized jobs, as well as speedups.

Motivated by the heightened dissatisfaction that followed the move to the new building, the imposition of productivity standards, and the threatened loss of benefits, a small group of office workers contacted Local 1401 of the Retail Clerks in the spring of 1975. An organizing committee targeted potential sympathizers and visited them at home to promote unionization. Once a majority of WPS workers had signed union cards, a representational election was scheduled for December of 1976.

WPS executives launched a campaign to undermine the unionization effort. Middle managers and supervisors were instructed to prevent union representatives from entering the premises and to reprimand employees for distributing union materials. Office workers received memos describing the negative aspects of unions, and the president of the company called meetings to discourage office workers from voting for the union. And management singled out union activists for harassment. "Management increased its pressure on the employees, picking at us for how we did our work," reported one union supporter. "They had the attitude that we were just underlings and don't we dare think otherwise."

The work force was divided about unionization. Afraid of

jeopardizing future wage and promotional opportunities, some office workers avoided union organizers. But among other employees, management's behavior and patronizing attitudes reinforced their need for a union. On the morning of the certification election, the company distributed a leaflet stating that the women were "insufficiently educated" to make an informed decision about unionization. The memo backfired: It pushed many of the undecided to vote for the union. As a result, Local 1401 won the election by a slight margin.[2] Union supporters celebrated their victory, but the narrowness of the vote put the union in a weak position.

WPS hired a law firm well known for aggressively challenging unionization—Seafarth, Shaw, Fairweather, and Geraldson—and appealed the election results to the National Labor Relations Board (NLRB).[3] The NLRB eventually decided in favor of the union but the appeal stretched out for almost a year, preventing Local 1401 from entering into contract negotiations with WPS until the fall of 1977.

The negotiations for the first contract were protracted and difficult. The outcome was a weak contract that gave the union workers a grievance procedure and salary schedule but entry-level wages remained low—between $2.65 and $4.78 an hour for most positions. In addition, vacation and sick-leave benefits were reduced, and a strong management-rights clause guaranteed the company exclusive control over job restructuring, work rules, and discipline procedures. Most important, the contract granted management an open shop: New employees were not required to pay union dues.

WPS Tightens Its Control

Over the next several years, WPS tightened its control over the union work force.[4] Scientific management provided the rationale for the establishment of REs throughout the firm. Explained one supervisor:

Time-motion experts came in with stopwatches. [They] analyzed each procedure—dictating a letter, opening envelopes and determining where the contents should go—[to get] a consistent step-by-step procedure. They would time individuals who had been doing it for a while, those who had just started, etc. Then they would take the average. . . . They had a system that was supposed to be foolproof: For every person, no matter what tasks they were doing, it was made up of so many small components. So they would add up the components and *voilà* here is a task and a reasonable expectancy figure based on those tasks.

Productivity determined promotions and raises. Management closely monitored new employees and often fired those who fell short on their REs during probation. "It was pretty common to dismiss people on probation," reported one supervisor. "An example was trying to be set for other employees that WPS was a hard-line company and would not put up with a lot of goofing around or not focusing on the job or not taking responsibility."

The REs provoked extensive dissatisfaction among office workers at WPS. The "scientific method" for arriving at the expectancies was unclear. "When management tries to explain how they arrived at the numbers," one woman stated, "they throw so many numbers at you that you [can't] figure out what they did." At bottom, workers perceived the expectancies as "unreasonable."

The REs imposed a rigid standard on a work process with unpredictable elements. The system failed to take into account the time required to process claims. "They might expect seventeen claims an hour for hospital claims," explained one woman, "but if you get a difficult claim, it might take you fifteen to thirty minutes to do it. Then you have to make up the time. You can't say you had a difficult claim and that is why your RE was low." In addition, no adjustments were made for computer malfunctions. "Sometimes the computer is slow and this isn't recorded in your RE," stated a second woman.

The REs created considerable stress among the office workers at WPS. "We know we are expected to do more and more work for the same pay," emphasized one office worker. "Hence, the stress level keeps going up." Office workers also saw the REs as dehumanizing. "If you could just answer the phone and close everything off and not have to deal with the REs which are degrading. REs tell you that you are dishonest and they need to monitor your work."

Along with the REs came a tightening of managerial control in other areas. The absenteeism policy was particularly harsh. If a supervisor suspected an employee of lying, she called the employee's home to verify her illness. Employees were harassed when they returned to work, and absenteeism was the one "transgression" that alone could result in dismissal. Supervisors also reprimanded employees for leaving their department and talking with co-workers. Management told new employees that they could be fired for leaving their work area. Supervisors closely monitored their employees' interactions and reprimanded those found conversing with their co-workers: "One woman was looking up a code and the supervisor came up in back of her and in front of everybody said, 'What are you talking about, don't you know you should be sitting at your desk? You've talked all day and hardly done any claims.' The women [responded that] their conversation was work-related. The supervisor said she didn't care, that they were supposed to be at their desks and if they had any questions, to come to her."

Managers and supervisors were erratic in their treatment of union workers. "Some girls get harassed for sneezing or looking up from their desk," one woman explained. "Others can [get away with talking] for an hour or two." Supervisors treated their subordinates like children, degrading them in front of their peers to assert their authority. "The attitude—the way they treat their employees—I've never been treated this way in all my adult life as a working person," exclaimed one woman with thirty-six years of work experience in factories and offices. A co-worker agreed: "[We] are treated very bad[ly]. One supervisor refers to all the women as 'kids.' She is in her early thirties and there are some women in her department who are sixty years old. This is degrading."

Older women were especially vulnerable to management

harassment. Under budgetary pressures from upper management to cut costs, supervisors used demotions, productivity expectancies, and reprimands to pressure older, more highly paid employees to quit. "The longer you work at WPS," stated one woman, "the less job security you have. They can get rid of old employees and get new ones for cheaper." Echoed another woman: "The older women are afraid. They don't understand women's rights or union rights. All they know is they have to have a job and that is all they can handle."

The company's tactics created a climate of fear at WPS. One response was to "break down." "If you intimidate them long enough," stated one union employee, "the only escape they have is to burst into tears. Not that that will get them out of it. But it is their way of dealing with all the tension they have within them because they can't let it out for fear of being charged with insubordination." Another response was to quit. "Anybody who could get out did," declared a second office worker. "And those who were left behind told them to come back and get them as soon as they could."

Resistance to Managerial Policies

Those women who were "left behind" resisted managerial policies in a variety of ways. Some women ignored the company policy that they remain at their desks. "People do take long walks to get a drink in order to get a break," one woman reported. "You will find women in the bathroom touching their toes to relieve the monotony." Others challenged the company rule against talking. "Once a week we sit there on company time and have a gab session," explained one office worker.

> We start out discussing work and then go into other topics. The supervisors eye us but we eye them back as if to say, "Come on and say something to us." The supervisors know they can't intimidate us. You have to cut loose occasionally. . . . [They] can't expect someone to sit at their desk eight hours a day and work constantly. You just can't. We

71

play on the status differences between ourselves and the supervisors who are lucky to have a high school education.

A second woman told a similar story: "You are supposed to
get permission to go to another department. People don't
mostly. Regardless of what the supervisor says, people talk
to each other anyway. It varies. . . . The more work there is,
the less talking. . . . You can talk and open mail without any
problems; people would probably open it faster if they talked
to keep their mind off the boredom of the work. People talked
mostly about their personal lives. If they are complaining,
they are talking about work."

Collective challenges to "tyrannical" managers were more
sporadic, but they did occur. Women in one department reported to upper management that their supervisor abused
her phone privileges and consistently returned late for lunch.
The result: "This supervisor got her hand slapped." In a second department, women waited to turn in their time cards
until one minute before the end of the workday, forcing the
supervisor to stay an additional half hour. And, in response
to an arbitrary policy regarding phone calls, the women in a
third department initiated a slowdown: "We aren't supposed
to get phone calls but occasionally someone is allowed to and
this is done to create friction between employees. The supervisor was purposely trying to make the union employees angry under the assumption that when angry, employees work
harder. However, sometimes it backfires and we work twice
as slowly . . . but then they get us with the REs."

The REs provoked various reactions. In a few instances,
women's strategies were collective. When the company suspended an older woman for reportedly "cheating on her RE"
the entire department refused to speak to the supervisor, an
action that helped to win a successful grievance settlement.
More common were individual strategies to overstate or
regulate an office worker's output. In departments where
work was performed manually, office workers kept their own
production records. This provided the women with an opportunity to inflate their productivity scores. "If they only knew

that what they are doing is cultivating dishonesty," stated one woman. "The very honest don't mark everything they should; the dishonest mark things they shouldn't. If I have questions about whether I should mark or not, I go ahead and do it."

Where work was automated, the computer tabulated the productivity scores. In that case, the only option for the office workers was to regulate their own output. "I tell new employees who are performing at 100–150 percent of the RE that if they keep it up," one woman explained, "management will expect them to maintain that level." The RE system also fostered competition among union employees at WPS. Supervisors rewarded workers who met or surpassed the standards and reprimanded those who fell short. To enhance their performance, some women overreported their output, hoping to get special recognition. This brought promotions to some individuals, but it increased the pressure on the rest of the women in the department.

For those employees with low REs, office workers sometimes responded with their own sanctions. Since low productivity could lead to department reprimands, resentment surfaced toward those who, as one woman put it, "screwed around": "People get upset because they are working and this other person isn't. They will put up with the other person not working for a while if there has been a trauma in that person's family but then there is a point where they think that is enough."

The Union Response

Local 1401 faced major obstacles to building a strong membership at WPS. The open shop required union representatives to "sell" the union to new employees. This was made especially difficult by management's practice of emphasizing to new employees that they didn't need to pay union dues to receive union benefits. High turnover contributed to the union's difficulties: Approximately fifty employees left the company each month. No sooner would the business agent sign up one group of office workers for union membership than another group of union employees would quit. Other problems stemmed from the perception that the union was responsible for the loss of benefits in the first contract. The union had fought hard to win favorable language during the first contract negotiations, but many office workers blamed the union for the "poor contract." The union's legitimacy was therefore in question.

The geographical separation of the office workers across several office buildings posed a further challenge. With growth in business, the company moved several of its departments to a second building in 1978. This made communication among union employees particularly difficult and fragmented the union's support. But management's recalcitrance confronted the union with the greatest obstacles. The company refused to settle union grievances. During the term of the first contract, the union filed almost two hundred grievances but, confronted with a management unwilling to negotiate, it dropped or lost most of them.

Six months before the second contract negotiations were scheduled to begin, the Retail Clerks merged with a much larger union—Local 1444 of the United Food and Commercial Workers (UFCW). As the union entered its second contract negotiations with WPS in the fall of 1979, a central priority was to gain a union shop. Without it, the union at WPS would forever be weak.

The second contract negotiations at WPS were especially difficult. The company harassed union employees, monitoring their phone calls, bathroom use, and conversations. Management's proposal for reduced benefits and a minimal raise was not received favorably. "When people found out [about the company's proposal], this made them madder than anything," one woman recalled. "They were looking for more, not less." In addition, the patronizing attitudes of the company bargaining team fueled the office workers' grievances. "Management would not deal with the women," reported one member of the bargaining team. "We felt so degraded listening to their attorney and representatives who would deal only with [the male union representatives]. . . . They would act as if there weren't a woman in the room and make remarks. They made derogatory remarks about the divorced women and treated you as if you were an absolute imbecile and not worthy of consideration."

The union called a meeting to recommend that WPS office workers reject management's contract offer. Approximately 400 out of the 550 union employees were in attendance at a meeting negotiating stewards described as highly charged: "It was a feeling that I had never experienced before. There wasn't even standing room. The women on the negotiating team had been telling jokes. [The president of the local] said, 'Okay ladies, everybody is in consensus that we're not going to accept the contract.' As we walked in, the members gave us a standing ovation and clapped and cheered. . . . When [the president] said that the negotiating team had suggested they reject the proposal, the place went wild." The vote was split. Two-thirds of the membership in attendance voted to strike if WPS failed to offer a better contract within ten days. One-third voted to accept management's offer.

Over the next week, some union workers prepared for the possibility of a strike. They removed job-related materials—manuals and coding notes—from their offices and made picket signs. "We had our picket signs ready," one woman reported, "and [we] were prepared to strike." But several factors undermined the momentum for a strike. The strike benefits of $40 a week seemed inadequate. "A lot [of employees] were worried because their husbands were laid off or they were divorced mothers," one woman explained. "They wouldn't have had anything to live on. . . . Strike benefits wouldn't have been enough." In addition, the membership was divided in its support for a strike. One hundred fifty workers were absent from the meeting on the night of the strike vote, and an additional 130 had voted against a strike. Finally, management's threats weakened the women's resolve. As rumors circulated that the company intended to hire nonunion replacements, the outcome of a strike became more uncertain. One strong union supporter thought to herself, "Oh great, in six months I'll be out of a job. I'm not going to strike."

Just before the contract expired, WPS proposed a union shop that would require all new employees to pay union dues. The company had met the union's central demand. Management also offered a better wage and benefit package. The negotiating stewards were hoping for a better contract, but they lacked the support to reject management's offer. "A lot of stewards were sitting back not very happy with the contract," one steward explained, "but the [union leaders] were the experts and people went along with their recommendations because they knew a lot of people who would vote strike would not picket." A majority of the union members voted to accept the contract.

WPS Hires Nonunion, Part-time Employees

Following the 1979 contract negotiations, WPS stepped up its assault on the union workforce. The cornerstone of the company's campaign was the recruitment of nonunion, part-time workers. The bargaining unit covered full-time employees, as well as part-time employees who worked more than twenty hours a week. A handful of nonunion, part-time employees had worked at WPS for several years. Because of their small numbers, Local 1444 did not see the nonunion, part-time workers as a threat. By early 1981, the company had hired hundreds of part-time workers who worked fewer than twenty hours a week and hence did not qualify for union membership.

WPS hired three types of part-time workers. The first group was hired through a WPS-owned subsidiary—Administrative Technical Services (Ad Tech)—to work as data-entry operators and mailing-service clerks. These part-time workers did not receive benefits, and their wages were lower than the union workers at WPS. Many of these part-timers, who were primarily women, worked the night shift. The erratic scheduling of work—some nights too much, other nights too little—made it difficult to meet the productivity standards.

And without any grievance procedures, the part-time workers had no protection from arbitrary management decisions
regarding raises and promotions. "Management said that all
of the night employees would get a raise," reported one part-
time worker. "But then only three to five people got them and
others were mad. Management said that the others weren't
making their quotas. People were told to call personnel if
they were dissatisfied. One woman who had worked there
for three years and was very dependable did call. And [the
manager] said that he didn't care how long she had worked
there. She was lucky to have a job and if she didn't like it, she
could quit."

Local 1444 tried to organize the Ad Tech workers, but its
efforts were unsuccessful.[5] The high turnover rate among the
nighttimers—many of whom were students, homemakers, or
workers with other full-time jobs—posed one obstacle to organizing. Not surprisingly, the company aggressively opposed the union's initiatives. Management isolated union
sympathizers and distributed memos describing "facts and
fictions about the union." The company also warned employees that if they signed unions cards they could be fired. Once
the futility of the organizing drive became evident, the union
abandoned the effort.

WPS hired a second group of nonunion, part-time employees to work as keypunch operators in its remote work center
in South Beloit, Wisconsin. The working conditions for the
mostly young, black women hired to work at WPS's remote
center were especially harsh. Paid minimum wage and no
benefits, few of the women received raises during their employment with WPS. Their productivity standards were high
and their work schedule erratic. Many keypunch operators
commuted long distances to work to be sent home after only
two hours; others were laid off for days or weeks at a time
with little notice.

In the fall of 1982, the union initiated an organizing drive
at the remote work center. Initially, support for unionization
was strong: A majority of the keypunch operators signed
union cards and an election was scheduled. Two factors

77

turned the tables, however. First, the Teamsters Union decided to try to organize these workers as well, thus dividing union support. And second, WPS aggressively challenged the unionization effort. The company distributed memos warning employees about the costs of a strike. One memo stated: "Employees go on strike and lose their jobs should the employer hire permanent replacements during an economic strike." The union lost the certification election by a wide margin.

The third and most controversial group of nonunion, part-time employees hired by WPS were the homeworkers. Before the 1979 contract negotiations, the company employed five home typists, but by 1981, over one hundred women were working for WPS as homeworkers. Among union employees, the homeworkers provoked considerable controversy. Some union workers expressed concern that the homeworkers were exploited. "My concern is . . . with how the homeworkers are treated regarding pay, benefits, etc.," stated one union worker, a divorced woman with two children: "I have dealt with crummy situations at work but it isn't as bad as some woman in her home with three crying kids and really needing the money and nowhere to go and no one to talk with. . . . You clean up the homeworker act and then maybe I'll talk to you about how beneficial it is to someone who needs it but right now, it is a rip-off, they are just using people."

Other union workers resented the homeworkers. One office worker described the homeworkers as a "privileged group": "I talked to one homeworker with grown children and just wanted something to do. . . . Must be nice not to need the money. . . . I find it hard to feel sorry for someone who needs pin money." A second union worker was more emphatic: "I absolutely have to have a job because I support myself. . . . If I had to chose between my having a job and a woman who has a husband with kids, I would chose myself. . . . If I don't have a job, I have nothing. I am against the homeworkers and definitely think there should be a ban [on homework]."

Local 1444 explored the possibility of organizing the homeworkers, but the company beat them to it. Supervisors warned homeworkers that union employees resented them for taking their work away and underscored the negative repercussions that could follow from unionization. The company's tactics, together with the high turnover and relative isolation of homeworkers, undercut the union's efforts. Few homeworkers were open to discussing the possibility of joining a union.

Union Strategies, 1979–82

The union emerged from the 1979 contract negotiations in a weak position. The union shop required all new WPS employees to join the union, but many of the office workers were estranged from the union. Once again they blamed the union for what they perceived as a poor contract. Union stewards thought that a female business agent might encourage the office workers to identify with the union. In early 1980, Local 1444 hired one to represent the office workers at WPS and to strengthen the bargaining unit at WPS. She scheduled training workshops for stewards and informal meetings to advise union members on procedures for filing grievances. In addition, the business agent brought in union engineers to retime the REs.

These initiatives did not go unnoticed by the company. Managers interrogated union activists, pressuring them to reveal information about union meetings. They instituted management-controlled "Employee Communication Committees" to circumvent the union and harassed the new business agent, escorting her around the building, from the cafeteria to the restroom, whenever she visited on union business.

This last strategy backfired. To some union workers, management's behavior represented a form of psychological warfare meant to warn union employees, "If we can do this to your business rep, just look what we can do to you." The union women, however, saw the business agent as a role model. One office worker commented on the satisfaction gained from watching the union representative "hold her ground": "[The new business rep] has had to deal with . . . harassment. . . . Management is scared of her because she has stood up more and shows up there all the time . . . to meet the stewards. It shakes them up to see her inside the doors. They get fidgety and stutter. She makes a point of being there for every little thing. It is funny to see a very cool manager stutter because she is in the lobby. I have seen this and I have to keep myself from laughing." A second woman agreed: "Since sex is around, it tickles the women that the new business rep got the best of one of the managers. He made a lot of mistakes in dealing with the union and she was quick to point them out; this led to the manager's losing points with the company. It tickles the people that the new rep has brains and guts."

Throughout 1981 and 1982, the pattern of management harassment continued. A dress code was imposed that prevented employees from wearing blue jeans, tennis shoes, T-shirts, tops with low necklines, and "extreme" hemlines. To some union workers, the dress code had one purpose: to reinforce managerial authority. Stated one woman: "The company imposed the code because they're interested in power, in imposing their rights." A second woman resented dress requirements that workers couldn't afford: "If management wants to pay us the wages where we could buy three-piece outfits, then I would willingly oblige."[6] A few women ignored the dress code and continued to wear blue jeans and long skirts. Management reprimanded the women and they responded by filing grievances.[7]

Grievances were also filed over production standards, absenteeism, and job requirements. When the company refused to settle the grievances, the union turned to the NLRB. The NLRB did direct the company to provide information to the union on production standards and nonunion, part-time employees, but on the most important issue the board sided with the company: The NLRB ruled that WPS had not hired part-time, nonunion workers to undermine the bargaining unit.[8]

During the 1982 contract negotiations, the company proposed substantial reductions in union benefits, most important the imposition of a 25 percent employee contribution to insurance premiums, the institution of a twelve-month waiting period in the vacation policy, and a wage freeze. The average wage at WPS in 1982 was $4.74. Union workers were very dissatisfied with the company's offer, but the economic recession made a strike unlikely. Stated one woman: "With the financial situation of most people, with layoffs in other industries, and because many [employees] are self-supporting, people will think a lot harder about striking."

In addition, the presence of nonunion workers at WPS had seriously diminished the union's leverage. Between 1979 and 1982, the size of the bargaining unit had shrunk by over one hundred employees, while the combined number of part-time workers had increased to more than four hundred. "The union didn't have any power," one woman emphasized. "Management had three years to cover themselves for the eventuality of a strike . . . to where management could tell the union to 'go to hell.'"

The union held its own in the 1982 contract negotiations. Most important, the union was able to protect the union workers' health-insurance benefits. It also gained stronger language granting workers the right to union representation during meetings with management and a wage increase of 2 percent to 6 percent, depending on the grade level. The most significant loss was the institution of a twelve-month waiting period in the vacation policy. The business agent felt that the negotiations turned out "as best as could be expected."

After 1982

By the mideighties—ten years after the beginning of the initial unionization drive at WPS—management-labor relations had stabilized somewhat. The company had accepted the union, albeit grudgingly, as evidenced by the willingness of a new labor-relations manager to inform Local 1444 of relevant changes in company policy. Perhaps WPS management no longer perceived the union as any threat.

The worst fear of the union—that the company would steadily erode the bargaining unit with nonunion, part-time workers—had not come true. In response to increased business, WPS had expanded both its nonunion and union work forces. The increase in their own numbers made union employees less anxious about their jobs, but the persistence of the part-time, nonunion workers undermined the union workers' morale.

The basic managerial approach at WPS remained unchanged. Close monitoring and negative reprimands characterized managerial treatment of union employees. Stewards continued to encourage union members to file grievances; those who did were sometimes empowered by the experience. But the attitude of the company stood as a powerful deterrent to the office workers' initiatives. WPS employees didn't have to look very far for examples of women who had paid the price for challenging the company. As one steward stated, "There [are] very few who aren't intimidated by the power structure at the company." Each month, forty to fifty office workers left their jobs. For the women at WPS, quitting represented a strategy of last resort.

Conclusion

This analysis of authoritarian management and conflict at WPS demonstrates the contradictory impact of coercive managerial practices on clerical activism. WPS was a classic authoritarian workplace, reminiscent of nineteenth-century despotic employers.[9] At this company, Taylorism and negative sanctions reinforced management's ultimate authority. Company policies consistently generated widespread dissatisfaction and initially provoked a successful unionization drive, but in the long run, the very managerial practices that alienated the clerical workers eroded their capacity for collective action.

A deterioration in working conditions catalyzed the initial unionization drive at WPS. Managerial harassment intimidated some office workers, but these efforts failed to over-

power the momentum for unionization. Following the certification election, the aggressive campaign undertaken by
WPS had mixed consequences for the union work force. On
the one hand, the tightening of managerial controls created
pervasive dissatisfaction with working conditions at WPS.
Complaints about the company were widespread, as were
employee initiatives designed to circumvent managerial
policies.

On the other hand, managerial harassment created a vulnerable work force, many of whom were afraid to challenge
the company. Not only did coercive working conditions
weaken the women's confidence in their individual ability to
confront management but managerial policies also undermined collective solidarity. Within departments, close supervisory surveillance and productivity pressures constrained
the office workers' interactions. The forging of ties across departments was that much more difficult.

The 1979 contract negotiations marked a turning point in
management-labor relations at WPS. As the linchpin of management's strategy, the hiring of nonunion, part-time workers weakened the union by providing potential replacements
in the event of a strike. In subsequent negotiations, there was
no evidence of a lessening of workers' grievances at WPS, but
the capacity of the clerical workers to mount a collective
challenge did diminish.

The office workers at WPS faced several barriers to collective action. First, the separation of employees across several
buildings impeded the development of social ties, requiring
the union to build support in several locations. Second, the
threat of replacement by nonunion workers undermined collective solidarity among the union workers. Third, weak support for the union diminished possibilities for creating ties of
solidarity outside of work. Finally, and most important, management repression intimidated the WPS office workers, led
to high turnover rates, and stood as a constant reminder of
the likely consequences of collective action.

A comparison of the Trust and WPS underscores that objectionable working conditions are a necessary but not suffi-

cient condition for clerical activism. At both companies, dissatisfaction with managerial practices was high, but a crucial difference distinguished the two settings. At the Trust, the office workers were able to exploit the ties between Trust management and its parent union to gain improvements in working conditions. The absence of any constraints on WPS management left WPS office workers vulnerable to management retaliation. That WPS office workers successfully unionized and held onto their union in the face of management assaults was a tremendous accomplishment. Still, this case stands as a sobering testimony to the challenges faced by office workers in authoritarian work settings.

NOTES

1. The data for chapter 3 were derived from fifteen semistructured interviews with office workers at WPS, six semistructured interviews with former managers at WPS, and several semistructured interviews with the business agents for Local 1444 of the United Food and Commercial Workers. The interviews with office workers covered work history, union background, family status, work experiences at WPS, and union participation. The interviews with former managers included questions on managerial policies, decisions, and attitudes, as well as questions on the relationship between the company and the union. Interviews with the business agents covered the history of unionization at WPS, management-union relations, grievances, and contract negotiations. The interviews have been slightly edited for grammar and punctuation. Additional materials for this chapter—union contracts, newspaper articles, and union leaflets—were provided by Local 1444 of the United Food and Commercial Workers.

2. A second union, the Office and Professional Employees International Union (OPEIU), was also on the ballot and received nine votes in the election.

3. Seyfarth, Shaw, Fairweather, and Geraldson is one of the largest and most successful anti-union law firms. Among other cases, the firm was linked to the events that surrounded the elimination of the union at the *Washington Post*, as well as to the events that undermined the Steelworkers' Union in Newport, Rhode Island. (See "The Heat Is on at WPS," *Free for All*, Nov. 5–8). More recently, this law firm was hired to advise Yale University regarding the union organizing drive by its clerical workforce (see "Yale

Strike on Hold," *In These Times,* Apr. 4–10, 1984). The most direct evidence that Seyfarth, Shaw, Fairweather, and Geraldson advised WPS management comes from the company's 1982 annual report to the state insurance commissioner listing payments of $177,676 to the law firm (WPS Annual Financial Statement, Wisconsin State Insurance Commission, 1982). Former supervisors, the business agents for the union, and union employees reported the presence of lawyers from the firm at bargaining sessions and arbitration negotiations.

4. Several of the union employees suspected that the tightening of managerial authority, together with the erratic supervisory behavior, reflected a managerial strategy forged in consultation with the law firm of Seyfarth, Shaw, Fairweather, and Geraldson. They based this assessment on memos found on supervisors' desks and on informal comments made by managers. The evidence indicates that the consulting firm was at least indirectly involved in supervisory training through consultations with upper-level managers regarding supervisory practices.

5. Initially, not all the night-shift workers were nonunion employees. After 1979, WPS management replaced union workers with nonunion workers as the former quit or transferred to day-shift work.

6. Not all the union employees shared this opposition to the dress code. One older woman expressed strong disapproval at the way the younger women dressed and complained that discussions about the dress code absorbed a disproportionate amount of time at union meetings. She stated that several of her friends had stopped attending union meetings over this issue.

7. See Janice Czyson, "Long Skirts Prompt Legal Battle," *The Feminist Connection,* Dec. 1982.

8. *UFCW Monitor,* Jan. 1982, June 1982, Dec. 1982.

9. See Michael Burawoy, *Manufacturing Consent: Changes in the Labor Process under Monopoly Capitalism* (Chicago: University of Chicago Press, 1979).

4

"Double Duty"

Work Experience and Strategies
of the Homeworkers
at the Wisconsin Physicians
Services Insurance Corporation

It is very stressful because you have double duty. You
have to take care of the kids and try to make these deadlines. . . . I found that with homework, I was always doing something and not doing anything for myself. . . . It
would have been much simpler for me to go out during
regular working hours and then come home to my kids
than what I've gone through.

—Homeworker, Wisconsin Physicians
Services Insurance Corporation

Beginning in the winter of 1980, the Wisconsin Physicians
Services Insurance Corporation (WPS) began to recruit
home-based workers as part of its strategy to hire nonunion,
part-time workers. By 1984, the company had hired approximately one hundred women to work at home processing insurance claims. A senior vice-president of WPS told the *New
York Times* that the homework program was initiated to "provide meaningful, gainful employment for the homebound."[1]
A closer look reveals that the homework program provided
WPS with a strategy for cutting costs, increasing flexibility,
and, perhaps most important, circumventing the union that
represented the in-house work force.

Compared to the office workers at the Trust and the in-
house work force at WPS, the homeworkers were unlikely

candidates for collective action. Through homework, women sought to fulfill their family commitments while retaining their ties to the labor market. Many homeworkers did find that employment with WPS fell short of their expectations, and common frustrations prompted homeworkers to develop friendship networks. These networks provided an outlet for women's grievances and a vehicle for developing strategies that circumvented company policies. However, the home-workers' capacity to act collectively was impeded by the transitional nature of their employment together with their isolation, their vulnerability to management retaliation, and the inaccessibility of labor resources.[2]

The Clerical Homework Program at WPS

Several motivations shaped WPS's decision to hire home-based women as typists, coders, and claims adjustors. First, the homeworkers provided a cost-effective method for adding staff to process high-volume medical and dental claims without expanding the office space. A recent increase in business at the company put office space at a premium. Second, home-workers provided a flexible work force for a company in an industry with peak and slack periods. WPS could hire part-time homeworkers and adjust their hours to the flow of insurance claims at the company. Third, homeworkers were less expensive than their in-house, unionized counterparts. In 1984, homeworkers were hired at $3.75 an hour, and, unlike the in-house workers, they did not receive automatic wage increases. By not paying for leave time or health and pension benefits, the company saved additional costs as well.

Finally, the substitution of nonunion homeworkers for union employees allowed management to bypass the union. As described in chapter 3, an acrimonious relationship between the company and the union had existed since the certification election in 1976. The conflict peaked in the fall of 1979 when the union employees voted to strike against WPS but later withdrew the threat when the company agreed to a contract with a union shop. Because it excluded part-time workers from the bargaining unit, the 1979 contract provided WPS management with an opportunity to circumvent the union. In 1980, WPS began to hire large numbers of part-time and temporary employees to work in the company offices, as well as women to work at home. One former manager described the thinking behind the part-time work force: "There [was] never a good atmosphere at WPS in terms of union versus management. The idea [of the homework program] was to expand outside of the union . . . [to eliminate union] staff without having to go through all the hassles with the union."[3]

The company recruited women with preschool or school-age children to work as homeworkers. Women with clerical and medical experience were preferred, and the home environment of a potential homeworker was of special concern. "You looked to see that they took care of themselves and their house," explained one former supervisor, "and then they would take care of their work." The applicant's plan for accommodating mothering and homework responsibilities was also considered. Experience with homeworkers whose children "spilled [food] on the claims materials" made supervisors wary of women unable to separate their household from their homework tasks.

Once hired, homeworkers completed a two-week training program at the company. Supervisors instructed small groups of homeworkers in the skills of claims processing—the interpretation and coding of medical diagnoses and procedures, the application of insurance guidelines, and the determination of insurance payments. Between 4:00 and 7:00 P.M., four days a week, a truck delivered a bucket of claims to the homeworker. The amount of work varied from day to day and week to week, depending on the work flow at WPS's main office buildings. The homeworker had twenty-four hours to complete the work except in the case of the Thursday night delivery, which left the homeworker with the weekend.

Homeworkers performed different tasks. Some women addressed envelopes, pulled staples from insurance claims, and typed correspondence. The majority were either coders or adjustors. Both of these groups first counted the claims to ensure that the total matched the number listed on the invoice sheet. Coders then transferred the appropriate codes for medical diagnoses and procedures from insurance manuals to insurance claims. Homeworkers who adjusted insurance claims also checked the diagnosis for each claim to make sure it matched the medical procedure and consulted insurance manuals to determine the cost of the service performed. They then recorded onto a code sheet the appropriate codes for the medical diagnosis, the medical service performed (e.g. checkup, surgery, or X-ray), and the charge for the medical service. At the end of the day, the claims adjustors and coders entered the total number of claims processed onto a ticket.

Until 1984, all of the homeworkers processed insurance claims manually—the only tools required were code sheets, pencils, and calculators. Beginning in 1984, WPS began to introduce personal computers to a handful of homeworkers. The delivery system didn't change, but some homeworkers received computer disks along with their insurance claims. Computer homeworkers entered data from insurance claims directly onto computer disks, thereby eliminating the step of transferring information from the insurance claim to the code sheet. Over the next two years, the company increased the number of computer homeworkers, but the majority of homeworkers continued to process claims manually. As a company that was automating its claims process very slowly, the distinction between manual coders and computer homeworkers paralleled the division between different groups of office workers in WPS's main office buildings.

The homeworker had only sporadic contact with WPS management. After the initial training, homeworkers were instructed to call their supervisor between 10:00 A.M. and 1:00 P.M. as questions arose. Supervisors communicated with homeworkers through memos outlining any procedural changes. They also sent homeworkers monthly audits reporting their productivity and error rates. Personal contact with supervisors was rare. Periodically, supervisors called meetings to update homeworkers on new procedures for processing claims. And once or twice a year, supervisors visited the homeworker to evaluate her performance.

Homeworkers received a maximum raise of 8 percent, and periodic raises were not automatic. Although this was not a piece-rate system, the primary factor affecting raises was productivity. Productivity was measured against the number of claims homeworkers were expected to process in an hour—the reasonable expectancy (RE). The homeworkers' attitudes and absenteeism also affected their raises. (Women who were frequently unavailable for homework received a high absenteeism score.) The highest paid WPS homeworker had worked at home for five years and earned $5.00 an hour. Most of the homeworkers earned $4.00 an hour or less.

The Motivations of Homeworkers

Contradictory motivations shaped the homeworkers' decision to seek employment with WPS. Women's responsibility for young children was an important factor. Many homeworkers saw their employment with WPS as a way to put their parenting commitments first. All but one of the homeworkers were married, and their average age was thirty-one. All of the women had children: 58 percent had preschool-age children, 19 percent had school-age children, and 23 percent had children in both age groups.

For some of the women, homework was consistent with traditional values about women's roles. "It sounds old-fashioned, but women are still the ones who raise the children," stated one homeworker. "After that, if a woman needs to get a job, preferably part-time, and if it is really necessary for a family, then that is alright. But I'm opposed when women get in and take jobs from men who really are the breadwinners. And I see men who can't get jobs . . . because affirmative action says you've got to hire this many women or blacks. Yet, I'm not opposed to working women. Women have to work. [But], the job is secondary to the family." And a second homeworker echoed: "I feel that women who are out there working don't have to be working. They are wanting more than they really need to live on. If they tone down their wants, they could make it without working. . . . I think that a woman with career aspirations should integrate that into her family life."

Many of the homeworkers were less ideological and more pragmatic. At this stage in women's lives, homework offered an avenue for fulfilling parenting responsibilities and earning an income. The yearly earnings of homeworkers ranged from $1,000 to $4,450 a year, with an average of $2,380. While their income was minimal, homeworkers calculated the money saved on gas and clothing. "I wouldn't consider this gainful employment," stated one homeworker, "but if you have children at home, you can dress in rags all day. . . . The work is brought right to your home and you don't have to spend money on gas or car insurance."

The money saved on baby-sitters provided an additional incentive to work at home: "I thought that hiring a baby-sitter for the amount of money I could make [by working outside the home] would be just crazy because you would be paying out just about everything you earned for a sitter." The average family income of homeworkers was $29,600, with a range from $12,000 to $50,000 a year. For women with lower family incomes, their earnings paid for groceries and rent, while those with higher family incomes helped to pay for their children's education, vacations, or household purchases.

Homeworkers also hoped that employment with WPS would offer an opportunity to retain their ties to the labor market. All of the homeworkers had high school degrees, 60 percent had some college education, and 28 percent held baccalaureate or nursing degrees. Most homeworkers had previously worked in the white-collar and service sectors as waitresses, clerical workers, teachers, or health-care workers. Some of the women were ambivalent about leaving the labor force for children. "Work is important," asserted one homeworker, "and it is hard giving up a job. I had to decide if I would push my career or be with my children." Homework offered a means, some women thought, for preparing to reenter the work force. Others hoped that the experience gained from adjusting claims at home might provide a route to job mobility. One woman underscored that she didn't want to start at the bottom again when she returned to the work force full time: "I didn't want people to think I have been sitting around eating potato chips and dip."

Finally, employment as homeworkers offered women a way to enhance their self-esteem as well as their bargaining power with their husbands. Some women felt devalued in their status as homemakers. "I was tired of everyone saying, 'Are you working now?' And I'd say, 'Yes, I work full-time. I'm home with my children.'" Homeworkers felt that WPS was placing a "value" on a homemaker's time. "There was somebody out there who was willing to hire us," stated one homeworker. "We're not just housewives—people with no minds—that are sitting home raising children. Somebody was giving us a chance to use our minds again and paying us to do it." Women also hoped that their homework income would provide a small measure of economic independence. As one woman explained, "I was always asking for money from my husband and I felt left out of everything. Then I thought, 'With homework, at least I'd have my own paycheck and I could do what I wanted to do with it.'"

Homework and Family Life

Women adapted their homes to the requirements of homework with varying degrees of success. Homeworkers with extra space transformed a spare bedroom or basement into a home office, sometimes with the help of husbands. Women with a separate room for claims adjusting could leave claims forms, calculators, and reference books out without worrying that a family member would disturb them. Others felt that the homework materials intruded into their households. Those with little space often used a kitchen table to process claims, requiring the constant packing and unpacking of homework materials for meal preparation. "When I started out," stated one homeworker, "I had a little area where I worked and I could put work aside and leave it out. By the time I left, I had a large box full of information and paper. [It] was cluttering up the family environment."

Some homeworkers appreciated the solitude of the work, particularly at first. Working at home offered a break from the petty difficulties encountered in the office. "I like regulating my hours," reported one woman. "You do your work and nobody is hassling you or watching you." A second homeworker characterized the appeal of working at home: "Being able to do it at my own time, setting my own hours. No one was watching . . . over my shoulder all the time, making sure I was doing it correctly." Another homeworker found that the arrangement allowed her to claim privacy: "I thought, this was one time of the day I can be alone, no one will bother me."

For other homeworkers, the feeling of "being cut off from the mainstream" was disconcerting. Women missed the social interaction of the office and looked forward to returning to an organizational work setting. "The isolation was awful," reported one homeworker. "I had always worked with lots of people. I liked being out in the office. . . . I felt out of it. I was like a recluse. I didn't know how women were wearing their hair. . . . That part was real hard." A second homeworker agreed: "At first, it was great. I thought, 'This is really it. This is fun. I can finally be home with my kids.' And I enjoyed being a domestic person. . . . After awhile, I think I started talking like the kids. I missed the interactions with other people. I missed doing what I like doing best, that is, being a secretary and being able to work with other people."

The invisibility of their work created problems for homeworkers. Friends and neighbors who presumed that homeworkers "weren't really working" didn't hesitate to call for a social chat, drop in for a visit, or send their children over to play. "Other women outside the home didn't look at you as working," reported one homeworker, "so they think of calling you any time of the day. It is so frustrating. . . . People think it isn't work, [but rather] a hobby."

Even spouses sometimes failed to regard homework as "real work." "It is hard because [my husband] doesn't see it as a job because I am home," stated one homeworker. "A lot of men in this world think that just because you are at home, you aren't doing anything. I think they should have their heads looked at." In a few cases, homeworkers themselves downplayed their work. When friends asked her if she was working, one homeworker responded, "No." Despite the homeworker's desire for a work-based identity, the marginal nature of home-based employment made family members, neighbors, and even the homeworker herself unable to see it as a "real job."

Women differed in their ease in juggling household, childcare, and homework responsibilities. Some women integrated the homework into their lives with little difficulty. "I don't mind homework," one woman with a preschool daughter explained, "because when I'm home, I can have the laundry going when I am doing my homework." A second homeworker expressed a similar assessment: "You really can't ask for more [than] to have the work actually brought to you and still be able to raise your children." And a third woman concurred: "On the whole, I didn't think you could beat it because you were getting minimum wage or just a little above, but you were still able to be at home with your kids and you could work it around your schedule."

But other women encountered difficulties balancing the demands of homework and family. Some husbands helped with housework or child care, enabling homeworkers to complete their claims adjusting, but this was unusual. For most women, claims adjusting was added onto their housework and child-care responsibilities, resulting in a long workday. Women with children in school could complete most of their claims adjusting during school hours. Those with preschool children at home processed the simpler claims when children were awake, leaving the more difficult ones for naptime, evening, and early morning. One homeworker's allocation of her time typified their strategies: "When I get the claims at night, I try to put in an hour while the kids are watching TV. Then I get up at 4:30 A.M. to work before the kids get up. . . . It is easier when nobody is around so my mind isn't wandering. . . . During the day, I turn on the TV and tell my pre-schooler to watch. . . . Then, when she takes a nap, I can work." A second woman described a similar work pattern:

> I would get up at 8:00 A.M., feed the girls, and try to straighten up a little bit. . . . At 11:30, I would feed the kids and then at 12:00, they'd nap. The entire time until 3:30 P.M., I would do claims. I'd do claims I hadn't finished the night before [while] getting ready for that day's pickup. I'd go for a ride with the kids. At 5:00, we would eat. At 6:00 sharp, my husband would take them downstairs and I would work. At 7:00 P.M., I would stop and get the kids in bed. Then, I would work until 10:30 or 12:30 at night. It was exhausting. I was never so drained. It hit and never went away.

Some homeworkers had no alternative but to let some of their housework go. Stated one homeworker: "As far as housework, the house was never in such bad shape." For women whose primary identity was bound up with home and family, this caused distress. "The [homework] is always on my mind at home," explained another homeworker. "I'd think, 'Oh, I have that work; I have to get it done.' If I could go [out to work], it would be done and I could come home and not think about it. I would just think about work around the home. Doing homework is real difficult for me because I think I should be doing homework when I'm doing the laundry and then I think, 'No, this comes first.'"

In particular, many women found the demands of home-work antithetical to the requirements of children. Claims adjusting requires concentration. Depending on their age and temperament, some children left their mothers alone to process insurance claims. Others did not. "I'd just get a claim done and [the baby] would get into something or he needed to be fed or held," stated one homeworker. "It is hard to hold a baby and do your work at the same time."

Particularly frustrating for many homeworkers was the negative effect of children's interruptions on productivity. Minutes spent responding to children's needs cut into the time allotted for each claim. "You are working at home with small children," reported one homeworker, "and you are always interrupted for 'Mommy can I have a snack? Can I have this?' You have to write down the time you stop and the time you start up again. I have time sheets a foot long [at] times." A second homeworker underscored the difficulty of balancing child-care and homework: "Contrary to public opinion, it is not easy [to do homework] because you have your kids that you have to work around. If children interrupt me, I have to start all over again and I have to absorb that time."

One of the ironies of homework was the cost it exacted on family relationships. Most homeworkers chose the work so they could care for their children, but to complete the work, they had to either keep their children occupied or ignore them. Over time, some homeworkers realized that they were snapping at their kids and homework was cutting into their family time. "It was stressful being interrupted and going back and forth to work and children," reported one homeworker. "I would say, 'Don't bother me now, mama is working.' That was not fair to my children because if anything comes first, my family does." Some children complained about the homework. "Mom is always at the claims," stated one child. "She can't take me anywhere because she's always at the bucket."

Many homeworkers concluded that the costs of homework were too high. "I was treating my children like they were getting in my way," stated one woman. "The main reason I quit my job at the bank was to be home with the children. [But] I was treating the job at WPS like a big career." Another homeworker summed up the contradiction inherent in homework: "The advantage is being able to stay home and the disadvantage [is] not being able to keep up with your parenting responsibilities."

Homework affected marital relationships as well. For some women, the homework earnings had a positive effect on their input into family decision making. As homemakers without incomes, women were reluctant to ask their husbands for money, but with the earnings from homework, women became more assertive. As one homeworker put it, "This job has given me my own independent power to make financial decisions." For another homeworker who would have preferred to work outside the home, the income earned from homework provided a degree of independence and autonomy: "My husband's preference is for me to be at home. . . . I would prefer to work out just for myself to get out. I first started working as a homeworker because I hated asking for ten dollars. I don't have much income, but it is nice not to always have to be asking."

At times, homework contributed to conflict with spouses. Some husbands objected that homework interfered with their wive's availability for companionship; other husbands resented their additional child-care responsibilities. "The money is not worth it," asserted one husband. "I can't stay down in the family room [with the children] one more night."

Homeworkers drew different conclusions about the effect of homework on their family lives. For some women, homework offered a perfect solution: There were sufficient hours in the day when their children were sleeping, playing, or occupied to complete the work. But others objected to the intrusion of homework into their households. "You can't leave your home-based problems behind," emphasized one homeworker. In the words of another homeworker, "The work was always hanging over your head. . . . I was always exhausted." And a third homeworker concluded:

> I felt that I was working full-time between doing the claims and even when my work was done, having to wait for the delivery. . . . The disadvantage to it for me personally was the feeling oftentimes of being trapped. . . . I would say to myself, "I'm only doing eighteen hours a week but I feel like I am doing this stuff all the time." . . . It was constantly hanging over me. . . . Even when my work was done, there was this new pile facing me for the next day. . . . I felt really tied down with it.

Job Satisfaction and Dissatisfaction

The women's satisfaction with the home as a work environment was integrally tied to their assessment of the working conditions associated with the WPS homework program. Homeworkers expressed mixed feelings about the daily work of claims adjusting. Particularly in the beginning, many homeworkers enjoyed their work. "I like the work," stated one homeworker. "Sometimes there is variety. Some [claims] are easy and others are difficult." A second homeworker concurred: "Work was a challenge. I would think, 'Gee, I can get these all done tonight and I think I got them all right. . . . These claims are easy and I can get them done in no time.'" But after mastering the skill of the job, many homeworkers found the work monotonous. "Once you get it," emphasized one homeworker, "it is like a factory or assembly-line worker."

Many women felt they deserved higher wages. "For a while, I rationalized [the low pay] by saying, 'I am saving money. They are saving money. It's a good deal for the company and it's a good deal for me so it balances out,'" stated one woman. "But I really think the company does get the better end of the deal. They are saving a lot more money than I am saving by staying at home." A second woman agreed: "They get a lot of work done for little money. And they know that. They are at an advantage because they don't have to pay benefits and they don't have to give any kind of decent raises. The women who stay have to stay and they know they've got them."

The reasonable expectancies (REs) were another source of dissatisfaction. The expectancies varied, depending on the type of claim a homeworker processed. Some of the homeworkers had no problem meeting the rate, but others concluded that the rates were unfair. "They make it sound like it is the offer of a lifetime," explained one homeworker, "but after you're hired. . . . they are going to squeeze everything out of you and then ask for more." Another woman characterized her employment with WPS as a "sweatshop": "It seemed to me that they were more interested in speed than anything else. They wanted to know how many claims you could process in a day. And the more you processed, the more they sent you."

The requirement that women be home for the delivery truck caused frustrations as well. Homeworkers were not paid for this waiting time. If the delivery truck arrived late, the homeworker sometimes missed a family activity. The erratic amount of work caused additional problems. Some homeworkers received a consistent amount of work from week to week, but others did not. "If they got behind in house, we went without work," stated one homeworker. "If they needed to get those claims it was always a call out . . . can we deliver some more? And they loaded us up." Under pressure to process all of the claims, homeworkers experienced stress. As one homeworker explained: "If you'd get six hours of work someday and you have two little kids at home and you only have three hours worth of TV, when are you going to get the rest of the work done? And you may have made plans. One of the advantages of being at home was the flexibility. And yet, you weren't really flexible when you had planned on getting three hours of work and all of a sudden they gave you six hours of work. . . . That really limited your flexibility."

Homeworkers also found supervisors unnecessarily rigid. Some supervisors made adjustments for the homeworker's family responsibilities, but others expressed irritation with homeworkers whose children interfered with their work. At one point, WPS sent homeworkers a memo offering suggestions for the scheduling of household tasks around the requirements of homework. Only in an extreme emergency, the memo stated, should women send claims back. Supervisory pressure to complete the work added to the stress experienced by homeworkers. "You are always meeting the deadline," one homeworker concluded. "You cannot live your life that way if you've got kids. I mean they get sick or they want to do things."

Networks and Strategies

The company's recruitment strategy encouraged homeworkers to forge friendship networks. By targeting several Madison neighborhoods for recruitment, WPS often hired women who already knew each other. Moreover, WPS actively encouraged homeworkers to recommend friends and neighbors to the company. The majority of homeworkers gained employment in the homework program through people they knew. "I was an Avon lady for a while," explained one woman. "And a lot of people I talked to in the neighborhood knew about the program because they had friends who did the work." WPS rarely needed to advertise for homeworkers because, according to one supervisor, "everyone in the homework program always knew somebody else [who wanted to work as a homeworker]."

The training program further contributed to the development of social ties among homeworkers. Homeworkers perceived the training as inadequate and disorganized. Confused and overwhelmed at the end of the training, homeworkers exchanged phone numbers and addresses before they returned home. "We wanted contact with each other for moral support," explained one homeworker, "[since] we were sent out in total darkness."

Homeworkers sometimes arranged get-togethers over coffee breaks or lunch. They also met at the local YMCAs, neighborhood churches, or family sports events. There, women discussed new recruits to the homework program and exchanged information about wages, memos, and evaluations. A desire to break the isolation of homework, chat about their children, or ask for advice also prompted homeworkers to communicate by phone.[4] "You really get close to these girls," reported one woman. "If you have problems, instead of having to call work all the time, you call one of them. And it was really nice." A phone call to another homeworker also helped to relieve the pressure. "By Wednesday, we were burnt out, crying our heads off," emphasized one homeworker.

Communication among homeworkers increased prior to the periodic meetings called by WPS to update homeworkers about procedural changes. In anticipation of meetings, homeworkers discussed their grievances with each other. Many of the meetings at WPS turned into gripe sessions as women complained about the low pay and rigid procedures, as well as the intrusion of homework into their family lives. The response from management was less than supportive. "[Management] would claim that they would hear the complaints," explained one woman. "Instead, it was their running roughshod over all the homeworkers." Stated a second woman, "When we left, we were always more disgusted than when we went to the meeting." Homeworkers often stopped at McDonald's to grab a bite to eat and let off steam.

These interactions encouraged homeworkers to develop a different interpretation of wages and working conditions from management's. Some managers thought that homeworkers were underpaid, but others viewed them as secondary wage earners from middle-class households. "Mostly, women were looking for a second income or something to do," stated one former manager. "They were bored. Most were middle to upper class. They did not need the money. Salary was not the issue." Homeworkers disagreed. Many homeworkers felt that they deserved higher wages for the skill and effort exercised in their jobs. One woman summed up the views of many of her co-workers: "What you needed to perform your jobs would have qualified you to make a lot more money."

Homeworkers also took issue with their lack of influence over company policy. WPS could change the rules and the homeworker had no recourse. "If the company says your performance must be higher to get a raise, you have no input into that," reported one homeworker. "You are totally out of the decision-making process." For many homeworkers, their grievances boiled down to a lack of respect. "That's one thing we don't really feel, that we are respected," emphasized one homeworker. "It's like they are doing you a favor by giving you this job and if you are not going to fill it, there is another woman out there who will take it."

Homeworkers responded in different ways to their working conditions. Some bit the bullet: "There were times when it was very stressful," stated one homeworker, "when I just wanted to throw that work right out the window. And then I'd say to myself, 'Just do it, it's just a job, earn the money, it's not worth worrying about.' . . . By taking the attitude that it's just a job, that's how I made it through." Although the unfairness of their working conditions was apparent to many women, few felt in a position to "create waves about it." Homeworkers therefore encouraged each other to "hang tough" with the admonishment, "It's just a job, you can put up with it."

Homeworkers did challenge management policies, however. The constant interaction among homeworkers ran counter to company directives, as did the decision by some women to take second part-time jobs. Homeworkers regulated their own hours in response to the unpredictability of daily work loads. Some women refused to process more claims than they could handle; others extended their hours beyond the nineteen and three-quarters maximum. Although the company didn't like the practice, WPS paid the homeworkers for the additional time.

Other initiatives focused on the REs. To improve their productivity, some homeworkers processed the easiest claims first and left the difficult ones to the end of the day. If the more challenging claims were returned unprocessed, so much the better for the homeworker. Other women paced themselves to extend their hours and prevent the company from raising the RE. "It wasn't to your benefit to do sixty an hour if the expectancy was thirty," explained one homeworker, "because then they would raise the expectancy and everybody would be expected to do it." Homeworkers also short-circuited the steps involved in claims processing. Since quantity was the company's focus, homeworkers decided that accuracy could be ignored. And in a few cases, women overreported their hours.

On multiple occasions, homeworkers individually registered their dissatisfactions with supervisors. Some complaints brought results: The production requirement was lowered in one case; a homeworker's raise was adjusted in another. More often than not, the homeworker's grievance was ignored. Management responded that if the homeworker disagreed with company policy, she could quit. A homeworker who complained was in a particularly vulnerable position. "The homeworkers aren't protected by any rules," explained one woman. "You are [therefore] at the company's mercy." Only one homeworker had been fired, but other homeworkers who challenged management authority were patronized, reprimanded, or denied work.

In a few instances, homeworkers tried to challenge the company collectively. When a group of homeworkers complained at a meeting about the REs the supervisor lowered the quota, but for the most part, homeworkers' collective initiatives were unsuccessful. In one case, a homeworker tried to organize her co-workers to demand higher wages. "I said," this homeworker reported, "'Let's all get together and say we have to get more money because we do all this work and it is [worth] good money.'" But her co-workers were unwilling to present a united front.

In a second case, conflict arose after a CBS news story revealed that WPS homeworkers were paid less than their in-house counterparts. Supervisors defused the homeworkers' grievance by pointing out that in-house employees paid for clothing, gas, and baby-sitters. And in a third case, several homeworkers voiced dissatisfaction when they learned that the company had hired new recruits for higher wages. Although many of the homeworkers were angry, few were willing to confront the company.

The labor union that represented the in-house workforce—Local 1444 of the United Food and Commercial Workers—did investigate the possibility of organizing the homeworkers, but the company did everything it could to block the union's efforts. Supervisors warned homeworkers during training sessions that union employees resented them. Supervisors also kept homeworkers out of the cafeteria to avoid any contact with union employees. While managers did not explicitly forbid homeworkers from interacting with union employees, they underscored the negative repercussions that could follow from unionization. The company's tactics, together with the high turnover and relative isolation of homeworkers, impeded union attempts to organize the homeworkers.

Despite management's actions, some homeworkers expressed an openness to labor unions that was surprising. One group of homeworkers talked seriously among themselves about their need for a union. "It was always a joke that we were going to form a union and really get after them for some of these breaches," emphasized one woman. "[But] sometimes it wasn't 'real jokey' when the women talked about forming a union. . . . We talked about [unionization] a lot. We didn't have any control over anything. . . . As far as getting our raises and things like that, we just thought, 'Well, if all the homeworkers were united, we could work it all out.'" However, the threat of management retaliation deterred the women from organizing. "I don't see how we could make demands for greater benefits and wages," underscored one homeworker. "We would be fired. If you questioned what they do, they would find some way to fire you."

Quitting offered a more expedient response to dissatisfaction with working conditions. Low wages, poor communication with supervisors, erratic work, and conflict with family responsibilities led most homeworkers to leave their jobs before their second-year anniversary. "The way WPS was set up when I was there," stated one woman, "there was no encouragement for you to stay there after you were no longer homebound. And they knew that. . . . When you had the opportunity to get out and get a job that paid more, you were going to quit." The discrepancy between the expectations and the reality of homework provided a common motivation for leaving. "Initially, at the time that I got the position," concluded one woman, "I was very happy about it because I had the job and I would be able to be home. . . . But that changed in the second year when I found my frustration level increasing and

I found that it just wasn't worth it any more trying to fight the group that was controlling us."

Conclusion

The WPS homeworkers were caught in a web of contradictions. On the one hand, these women accepted their place in a traditional division of labor that assigns to women primary responsibility for the household and child care. Against the backdrop of a strong commitment to their family roles, homeworkers sought a source of secondary income. But on the other hand, many homeworkers recognized the limitations of their family status and sought to increase their options. Employment with WPS offered an opportunity to enhance their feelings of self-worth and their future possibilities in the labor market. More than a means for coordinating their multiple responsibilities, homework promised an avenue for expanding women's alternatives.[5]

For many women, the experience of homework fell short of their expectations, as the home proved to be a less than satisfactory workplace. Instead of a flexible work arrangement, homework brought with it rigid company procedures, erratic work loads, and unsympathetic supervisors. As women attempted to adjust their family lives to the requirements of their homework schedules, children and husbands sometimes protested. Homeworkers found themselves caught between their family obligations and their homework deadlines. Nor did homework fulfill its other promises. The income earned from homework helped to provide women with an independent identity but the marginal nature of the work reinforced its invisibility. With time, it became evident that homework would not provide a stepping-stone into more highly skilled and remunerated positions.

As with the office workers at the Trust and WPS, a shared work experience among homeworkers provided a basis for the development of social ties. The extent of these friendship networks was unusual among homeworkers, who are typically isolated from other women in similar situations. Ironically, it was the recruitment policies and training programs of WPS that inadvertently fostered homeworkers' friendships as an outlet for their isolation and a source of advice for work-related problems.

Women's social ties also encouraged a collective assessment about working conditions and provided a resource for developing work-based strategies.[6] In only a few instances did homeworkers systematically challenge their supervisors. Homeworkers did, however, employ informal strategies—which ranged from setting their own work pace to quitting—for negotiating with managerial policies. With a large pool of homebound women eagerly awaiting the positions vacated by dissatisfied homeworkers, these initiatives posed little threat to managerial prerogatives at WPS. They nevertheless demonstrated that these homeworkers were actors who shaped their own responses to the constraints of work and family.

What prevented the homeworkers from mounting an effective, collective challenge to managerial policies at WPS? In part, the homeworkers' family commitments and temporary status weakened their resolve. Many homeworkers did express a consciousness about the problems with the homework program at WPS, and a few expressed strong commitments to equal opportunity and pay equity. Most of the homeworkers, however, viewed their WPS employment as transitory and subordinate to their family responsibilities. Had the WPS homeworkers intended to work indefinitely as homeworkers, their accumulated grievances might have sparked a collective organizing effort. But as it was, the temporary nature of the homeworkers' employment reduced their motivation to act.

A second barrier to collective action for the homeworkers was their isolation. True, the women's geographic proximity encouraged friendships that helped to foster a critical assessment of the homeworkers' working conditions, but to organize the home work force at WPS would have required the development of broad social ties across the multiple small groups of homeworkers who knew each other. The high turn-over rate among homeworkers undermined this possibility. And the two factors that typically encourage the develop-ment of strong ties of solidarity among workers—a central work setting that provides opportunities for workers to com-municate with each other and a labor union with resources to underwrite workers' organization—were absent.

The case of the WPS homeworkers demonstrates the obsta-cles to organizing for workers isolated in their homes. These women encountered many of the same problems as their counterparts who worked inside the company at WPS: pro-ductivity pressures, authoritarian supervisory practices, and rigid company policies. The central difference between the circumstances of the in-house work force and the homework-ers was their work setting. The concentration of the in-house workers into large departments brought them into daily con-tact with each other, even while supervisory surveillance constrained their interactions. Homeworkers did have op-portunities to interact with other homeworkers without the knowledge of WPS supervisors, but the daily requirements of homework, child care, and homemaking limited these inter-actions. More important, the homeworkers' isolation made them particularly vulnerable to management retaliation and made gaining access to union resources—the one factor that provided a small measure of protection to the in-house work-force at WPS—almost impossible.

NOTES

1. Bill Keller, "At the Center of the New Fight: Home Work," *New York Times*, May 20, 1984.
2. Most of the data for chapter 4 are based on interviews with five current homeworkers, twenty-one former homeworkers, and three former managers involved in the clerical homework program at the Wisconsin Physicians Services Insurance Corporation (WPS). There is undoubtedly some bias in the data because homeworkers were contacted through newspaper ads and recommendations from other homeworkers. They also were paid by the hour for their inter-view time. The open-ended interviews with homeworkers covered

work history, motivations for seeking employment as homeworkers, attitudes toward work and family, experience of working as home-workers, friendship networks, attitudes about the homework pro-gram, and strategies for responding to their work and family situa-tions. The interviews with former managers included questions on managerial responsibility for the homework program, advantages and disadvantages of homework, and perceptions of management-union relations. The interviews have been slightly edited for gram-mar and punctuation. Additional materials for this chapter—legal documents, labor contracts, etc.—were provided by Local 1444 of the United Food and Commercial Workers.

3. The factors shaping WPS's decision to recruit homeworkers re-sembled those of other companies. The one difference is that most companies with homework programs for clerical workers are not unionized. See Cynthia B. Costello, *Home-based Employment: Im-plications for Working Women* (Washington, D.C.: Women's Re-search and Education Institute, 1987).

4. For another discussion of the isolation experienced by home-workers, see Kathleen Christensen, *Women and Home-based Work: The Unspoken Contract* (New York: Henry Holt, 1988).

5. For an analysis of the ways in which women's family status shapes their work strategies, see Myra Marx Ferree, "Between Two Worlds: German Feminist Approaches to Working Class Women and Work," *Signs* 10 (Spring 1985): 517–36.

6. Feminist scholars have recently analyzed cases where wom-en's shared domestic responsibilities nurtured networks that pro-vided resources for work-based strategies. For example, see Temma Kaplan, "Female Consciousness and Collective Action: The Case of Barcelona, 1910–1918," *Signs* 7 (Spring 1982): 545–66, and Ardis Cameron, "Bread and Roses Revisited: Women's Culture and Work-ing-Class Activism in the Lawrence Strike of 1912," in *Women, Work and Protest: A Century of U.S. Women's Labor History*, ed. Ruth Milk-man (Boston: Routledge and Kegan Paul, 1985), 42–61.

5

"Like a Family"

Corporate Benevolence and Participatory Management at the CUNA Mutual Insurance Society

> I can remember being a little girl and saying, "When I grow up, I want to get a job at CUNA!" Everybody knew it was a good place to work, just like Oscar Mayer's.
>
> —Office Worker, CUNA Mutual
> Insurance Society

Compared to the Trust and WPS, the CUNA Mutual Insurance Society (CUNA Mutual) enjoyed a reputation as a good place to work. Whereas the other two companies pursued an authoritarian approach, CUNA Mutual adopted a human-relations managerial style that offered positive incentives for employees to identify with the firm. In its early years, the company provided better wages, benefits, and promotional opportunities than were available elsewhere. Together, the company and the union forged a partnership that helped to create a loyal work force. When changes in the company's competitive position led to the automation and reorganization of work, employees began to voice dissatisfaction with their working conditions. The company responded by introducing participatory policies to improve employee morale and productivity, while employees moved to democratize the union and form the Women's Association. These collective initiatives represented a break with the past, but neither posed a serious challenge to managerial control at CUNA Mutual.

109

An analysis of CUNA Mutual provides a valuable contrast to the Trust and WPS. At these other two insurance companies, objectionable management practices provoked clerical grievances that, when conditions were right, led to collective action. Where management's policies were overly dominating and coercive, however, collective action was stifled. The CUNA Mutual case demonstrates that a human-relations managerial style can also inhibit collective action, at least of the militant type. By providing positive incentives to its employees, CUNA Mutual largely succeeded in creating a satisfied work force. Workers had ample opportunities to develop social networks at work and within their employee organizations without fear of management repression. But with working conditions superior to other companies in town, CUNA Mutual employees had little motivation to pursue militant collective action.[1]

Benevolence and Loyalty at CUNA Mutual

CUNA Mutual was formed in 1935 by the Credit Union National Association (CUNA) to provide life-savings and loan protection to members of credit unions. In its early years, CUNA Mutual was closely tied, both philosophically and organizationally, to the credit-union movement. These ties shaped the ideology and working conditions at CUNA Mutual.

The first North American credit union was established in 1901 as a self-help organization to encourage savings and extend loans to working people. Credit unions were an outgrowth of the corporate liberalism of the period, best exemplified by Edward A. Filene, the chief executive officer of Filene Department Stores and the financier of the first credit unions. For Filene, credit unions offered a way to incorporate the working class into a mass-consumption society: "[Filene] believed that the future of our mass production system lay in making credit available to the masses and he believed that credit unions could achieve this."[2]

By 1934, there were 2,400 credit unions in the United States, and the Credit Union National Association (CUNA) was formed. A year later, the founders of CUNA decided to form the CUNA Mutual Insurance Society to provide savings and loan protection to credit-union members. The society's founders extended the "democratic ideology" of the credit-union movement to the new insurance society: "We were in full agreement that CUNA Mutual should, for all time, be of, by, and for the people," stated one of the society's founders. Edward A. Filene provided the initial capital for CUNA Mutual and became the company's first president, overseeing a board of directors that included two lawyers, three postal employees, a firefighter, a packinghouse worker, and a telephone-company employee.[3]

From 1934 to 1956, CUNA and CUNA Mutual operated under one joint administrative management. The institutional ties between the two organizations gave CUNA Mutual privileged access to credit-union members and insulated the company from the competitive pressures characteristic of the insurance industry. However, the company depended for growth upon the extension of savings and loan protection to new credit unions and the provision of new insurance services to existing credit unions. As a result, CUNA Mutual grew slowly, and its total work force numbered only sixty employees in 1950. Even after a substantial spurt in business during the fifties, following the postwar boom in the formation of credit unions, CUNA Mutual employed fewer than two hundred workers in 1960.

Recruited from credit unions, the company's first executives adapted the credit-union philosophy of the period, exemplified in the slogan "the brotherhood of man," to the CUNA Mutual context. Conscious attempts were made to create a "family" atmosphere at the company in the early years. The company sponsored extracurricular activities—a company softball team for the men and a choral group called "CU Notes" for the women. The wage and benefit package was superior to most employers in the city and job ladders provided opportunities for promotions from within. And, top

111

management went out of its way to develop personal relationships with its employees.

A claims examiner hired in 1948 nostalgically remembered this period: "A real 'family' relationship existed between management and employees. I remember when . . . the managing director in the late forties and early fifties would send a red rose to each female employee on her birthday. A generous, well-liked man, he would occasionally stop at the bowling alley after work, which was a popular social activity for many of us. Afterwards, he would take us all to eat." A manager hired in the midfifties shared similar recollections: "In the beginning, closeness just happened. I knew everybody in the company by their first name. . . . It was a small office . . . and people were very, very close. . . . In the beginning, it was like a family."

The employees at CUNA Mutual were represented by Local 39 of the Office and Professional Employees International Union (OPEIU), a union that helped to forge a "working partnership" between management and nonmanagement employees. The union was brought in by management in the late thirties in response to pressure from credit-union members who were themselves trade unionists. Essentially, the union at CUNA Mutual functioned as a company union: With the exception of the top executives at the company, all management and nonmanagement employees were members of the union. In the late forties, federal law stipulated that all managers except work-flow supervisors be removed from the bargaining unit. This left professional, technical, and clerical workers in a union that continued to operate as an arm of management for decades thereafter.

At CUNA Mutual each group had its place in the corporate family. At the head of the family were the top managers, who integrated their employees into the company through protective and benevolent policies. As long as the company rewarded them with material benefits, most employees accepted their subordinate position in the family and defined their interests as synonymous with management's. The union helped to cement the relationship between management and nonmanagement employees by smoothing over conflicts. Starting in the sixties, the expansion of CUNA Mutual brought changes in work organization that threatened to disrupt the positive atmosphere at the company.

Reorganization and Dissatisfaction

In 1960, CUNA Mutual formed a property and casualty company, followed in 1962 by the establishment of an international office to service credit-union members in other countries. A decade later, CUNA Mutual became the fourteenth largest life insurance company in the United States with a total work force of five hundred employees. The introduction of a credit and disability insurance line in 1976 resulted in the hiring of additional employees. By 1980, CUNA Mutual employed 1,300 workers in its Madison office: 400 management and 900 union employees.[4]

These two decades brought changes in the company's market position. Up until the sixties, CUNA Mutual enjoyed a near monopoly in its access to credit unions. By the early seventies, other insurance companies had entered the market. With industry deregulation in the early eighties, banks and multiservice corporations (e.g., Sears) began to offer insurance to credit unions as well. These new challenges to CUNA Mutual's competitive position pushed management to develop new strategies for increasing efficiency and productivity.

Like other companies in the finance industries, CUNA Mutual decided to streamline and automate its work process. In 1960, the accounting and billing systems were transferred to a newly formed data-entry department. With the introduction of an on-line IBM system in 1965, the word-processing department replaced the stenography pool, and the claims departments transferred their insurance files onto computer disks.

CUNA Mutual automated more slowly than other firms of its size, largely due to the heterogeneity of its product lines, which included life, auto, and health insurance.[5] For many products, the low volume didn't justify automation, but after the midseventies, the growth in business precipitated rapid automation: Electronic mail was introduced to improve communication across departments and regional offices, and personal computers were installed to facilitate financial projections and managerial decision making.

Automation brought mixed results for CUNA Mutual employees. For those workers who lost responsibilities, such as accountants, the changes were unwelcome. Before 1960, accountants used account ledgers and bookkeeping machines to maintain their records. With the introduction of a data-entry department, keypunch operators started to enter and maintain accounting records. Afraid that this change would lead to reduced control over work or layoffs, accountants objected to the computers and asserted that "the computer [would] never do the work as [they] did."

For the keypunch operators (or data-entry operators), dissatisfaction arose for other reasons. Data-entry work was repetitive and monotonous. Not surprisingly, a survey conducted at CUNA Mutual in 1980 found the greatest dissatisfaction among those employees who performed the most mechanical and repetitive of jobs. "What does a keypuncher do for seven hours?" complained one data-entry operator. "She sits there and she goes insane and she puts out as much work as possible. It's just like being a steady typist. You do nothing except move your fingers. . . . It is a very boring job."

Data-entry work was stressful. As was the case at WPS, CUNA Mutual established productivity expectancies for its data-entry operators. Based on department averages, management set expectancies for each job and evaluated the operators on the basis of their productivity. Some data processors adapted to the expectancies by setting their own goals. "It's a challenge once in a while when you can set a goal for yourself," one operator explained. "You can feel that you want to get so much done and say, 'I'm going to get all this done today.'"

Other operators found the expectancies oppressive. "I

didn't find working for eight hours keypunching stressful," one woman explained.

> What was stressful was knowing that every keystroke counts. You are working on a machine that tells you exactly how much you are doing in an hour. You get up and go to the bathroom twice and you lose 2,000 strokes. . . . If your strokes were down and they felt you were talking too much, you got reprimanded. In some cases, people were talking. In other cases, not so. Sometimes, you had a bad day. Sometimes your mind is not on your work. If your children are sick or something is going on in your life, you are thinking as you are punching. And then you are going to slow up because you lose track.

A second operator expressed a similar grievance: "The boss wants real high productivity. But some of us women figure we can only keypunch so fast. We can't make our fingers go any faster than they want to go. So we try to get out what we can get out. . . . The managers think we can do more but we feel we are doing what we can do. . . . Every once in a while during break we bring up the issue of production. We say we can only do what we can do."

There was an important difference between the productivity expectancies at CUNA Mutual and WPS. At WPS, the expectancies were the centerpiece of an overall system of management coercion. Many WPS employees were literally terrorized by the expectancies: They feared for their jobs if their productivity fell short. At CUNA Mutual, the expectancies were the source of pressure and frustration, and sometimes low productivity brought reprimands, but, for the most part, managers at CUNA Mutual did not employ punitive sanctions with their employees. Consequently, the office workers, although often disgruntled with the pace of their work, were not fearful.

CUNA Mutual also put a high value on training and provided opportunities for the office workers to enhance their computer skills. Consequently, many office workers were positive about the computers, especially in the word-processing department, where a limited job ladder provided women with the chance to move up. The entry-level position required the routine typing of prerecorded letters. Office workers saw this job as boring and unchallenging. "The only thing in the department I'm not fond of is prerecorded letters," stated one woman. "I tend to lose interest. I do enjoy typing. . . . I like to spell the words. I am real interested in the science of spelling. I would hate to lose that skill. In prerecorded letters, you do lose the skill because mostly you just fill in the variables and you can use the spelling program."

More challenging were the jobs that required the transcription, editing, and composition of letters. "I have to be able to think and read and type at the same time," one woman explained. "I have to know grammar and spelling. Even though it has a spell function, it doesn't check grammar. You need to have editing skills—to shorten up a paragraph and edit out redundancies. . . . I put myself in the position of the person who is going to get the letter. I want it to be understandable and be right to the point and not have to guess what the person is trying to say."

Still, the options for clerical workers in the word-processing department were limited. Once promoted to the top of the ladder, the word processor was stuck. "If you like being a word processor and like the equipment," one woman commented, "there is no place to go unless you want to change the focus of your career."

As is often the case with large companies, office automation brought with it reduced opportunities for promotions among clerical workers at CUNA Mutual. The reorganization of work into specialized departments of data-entry operators, word processors, and claims adjustors eliminated one of the central avenues for mobility among clerical workers. Up until the seventies, women hired for entry-level clerical positions could anticipate promotions into more highly skilled jobs, such as private secretarial positions. The shifting of tasks once performed by secretaries, such as typing and transcribing, to discrete departments reduced the number of secretarial jobs and lessened the likelihood that clerical workers would become secretaries. One consequence was a decline in employee loyalty at the firm. "The typical . . . employee is significantly different from the thirty-year veteran," reported one executive. "Anyone who came in thirty years ago worked their way up and those who didn't, did very well salary-wise. . . . You find women who have worked for twenty to thirty years [at CUNA Mutual] and are adamantly loyal. . . . My employees under thirty [years of age] are not disposed to have the same career attitudes of patience that the employee had thirty years ago."

Participatory Management

In the late seventies, CUNA Mutual executives were looking for new approaches to increase the productivity and job satisfaction of their employees.[6] Work teams were implemented on a limited basis. In the data-processing department, management reorganized the work process into teams and allocated responsibility for monitoring the operators' output to team leaders. Management thought the work teams were very effective. "Everyone has reacted great to this system since it started," reported one manager. "I think work gets out faster. Most of them like it; some don't. They like it due to the autonomy. You give them more responsibility and they accept more responsibility."

Data processors were more mixed in their reactions. Women gained autonomy from direct supervision, but in exchange, they became responsible for monitoring their own output. Since the output of the group was evaluated along with each individual's output, each woman had a stake in her co-workers' performance. In some cases, this led to greater cooperation among data-entry operators, as faster workers compensated for slower ones. "There are some girls who are really fast," reported one woman. "Sometimes, if one girl is really slow, it may affect the others but they try to work around her and have others compensate." In other cases, work teams pressured slower workers to speed up. "If a woman is slower, then that is a problem because others have

117

to take up the slack," one woman explained. "It is a little aggravating if someone is slow . . . it slows up the process."

The work groups affected only a handful of workers in the data-processing department, but quality circles involved almost every worker at CUNA Mutual. Quality circles were first introduced at the company in 1981. A year later, sixty quality circles were meeting on a regular basis. Modeled on a participatory approach first introduced in manufacturing companies, the quality circle program invited employees to recommend changes in policies and procedures that could increase productivity and job satisfaction.

Management had several objectives with the quality circle program: to increase productivity; to improve the quality of work life through employee enrichment and the development of employee "ownership" of their job activities; to increase participation of the entire organization in problem solving, job design, and methods improvement; and to increase the enthusiasm, morale, and loyalty of the workforce.[7] "The idea," reported the director of the quality circle program, "was that if employees were happy with their jobs, they would feel committed and help management do the work in the smartest way."

Many of the quality circles were successful. Employees offered suggestions for streamlining or reorganizing work and managers responded by initiating changes. But in some cases, nonmanagerial workers proved resistant to participating in quality circles, especially when they thought that cost-cutting suggestions might jeopardize their jobs. A newly created job rotation pool protected against layoffs, but employees were suspicious that the reorganization of work could lead to the elimination of their jobs.

Employees sometimes raised issues considered outside the bounds of the quality circle program. They complained that the measurement procedures requiring workers to tabulate their own output were reminiscent of "kindergarten." Other grievances focused on the "management-by-objectives" program that rewarded managers, but not union workers, for attaining productivity goals.

118

One unforeseen consequence of the quality circle program was managerial resistance. By involving union employees in departmental decision making, quality circles challenged managerial prerogatives. As a result, some managers felt threatened. The company resolved this problem by directing managers to limit the extent of employee participation in their departments.

The implementation of quality circles in the word-processing department revealed the dynamics that resulted from the program. Management selectively responded to recommendations of the office workers in the department. For example, word processors received little support for their complaints about particular supervisors. "There was an instance where personality-based dissatisfactions were discussed," one manager explained. "Managers tried to curtail this because this isn't what [quality circles] are for. Quality circles are to improve how you do your own work in your department and how you work with other departments." Nor were managers any more sympathetic to clerical dissatisfaction with the productivity standards. Stated one manager: "Anybody who feels threatened by monitoring isn't doing their job. The person who wants to talk a lot has a tendency to feel threatened. But the person who is doing [their] job is not threatened."

Word processors' suggestions for reorganizing work to increase the variety and mobility in their department met with greater success. Management introduced a job-enrichment program that trained the word processors in the skills required to perform each of the jobs within a grade level. In addition, management instituted a job-progression system that added another grade level to the department. Neither of these changes significantly expanded the job opportunities within the department, but they did provide a measure of variety and challenge that didn't exist before.

For the word processors, the quality circle program produced an additional benefit: Communication among the women led to the development of a sense of pride in their work. As they discussed their jobs, the women began to identify their skills as well as management's tendency to devalue their work. "When I first started, word processing was thought to be by people outside the department as a base-ment-level position," one word processor explained.

> We had no autonomy. So people had no self-esteem. This has undergone a complete change. . . . Quality circles al-lowed the girls to talk with each other. . . . [The managers who send us letters to type] think that women can type it up just like that and be done. A lot of times you can't. . . . Managers couldn't even figure out how to turn it on. . . . To us, it's a piece of cake. . . . The girls [let] each other know they do an important job and they do it very well and would thank others not to think of it as unimportant.

The limits to the quality circle program were demon-strated by the word processors' exclusion from decisions regarding new equipment. Without consulting the word pro-cessors (or the managers in the department), top manage-ment decided to introduce a new computer system into the department. One word processor underscored that the com-pany should have involved the office workers in the decision:

> We were all dissatisfied because we had just finished learn-ing the new machine and we were content and somebody else decided it had to change. The new machines don't even do half the things the others did. Somebody else said, "You are going to get these machines and don't have a say about it." I thought, "Why can somebody else say that when they don't even work on our work? They don't even know the kind of work we do." . . . I wish we were involved in equip-ment decisions.

Employee Initiatives

In the late seventies and early eighties the democratization of the union and the formation of the Women's Association signaled the breakdown in corporate benevolence at CUNA Mutual. With the company no longer providing the same level of incentives, employees sought to develop organiza-tions that could better represent their interests. In addi-tion, the promotion of employee participation through the quality circle program indirectly encouraged employees to strengthen their own organizations. And in the case of the Women's Association, the feminist movement encouraged working women to form their own advocacy oranizations.

Dissatisfaction with the status of the union began to surface in the late seventies. For almost twenty years, one woman had maintained control over the union. Paid by management, this chief steward appointed her own stewards, set the agenda and ran all union meetings, and met personally with the president of the company to resolve union-management problems. The acceptability of this arrangement came increasingly into question, especially as union workers sought avenues for enhancing their bargaining power with management. As a result of the close relationship between the company and the union, one woman explained, "the [union workers] didn't understand what the contract said. . . . they didn't understand that the union was there to help them . . . that if something went wrong, the union was there to back them up rather than have management always win."

In the fall of 1980, a small group of women initiated a campaign to democratize the union. The union quickly polarized into two camps: the "loyalists," who wanted to retain the existing union structure and the "reformers," who sought broader participation in the union. The "reformers" advocated for regular elections of union officials, elimination of a company salary for the chief steward, and greater communication between stewards and rank and file members. In a union-wide election, the "reformers" won. What followed was a second election for a new chief steward and twenty-eight representational and negotiating stewards.

The democratization movement made it clear that the union no longer saw itself as an arm of management. With the union's assertion of its autonomy from management, the company created a new position to oversee management-union relations—the vice-president of employee relations. This signaled a shift in the company's approach to managing the union. "It has become more difficult to maintain the caring posture of the company," one executive explained. "I don't want to use the word *paternalistic* but some would. . . . [This is] more difficult to maintain as the company has grown. It is more difficult to maintain a cooperative stance. It is more difficult for the union to maintain its 'obedient family posture' . . . [as] the demands of the represented employee change."

The tone of the 1982 contract negotiations—the first following the election of the new union leadership and the hiring of the vice-president of employee relations—was different from previous negotiations. Both sides were more aggressive during bargaining sessions. The union was able to improve its wage and benefit package, but management imposed a stricter absenteeism policy. No longer were management and union partners in negotiations; both sides had interests to protect.

The changes brought by the democratization movement should not be overstated, however. The union retained its commitment to resolving conflicts with management amicably, and the leadership accepted management's authority in many areas. Securing the rank and file's commitment to the company remained a central function of the union. For example, when management informed the union leadership that unless the company's profit margin increased layoffs could result, the chief steward asked union members to consider a reduced work week. One union employee objected to the union's acquiescence: "Who are they cutting back on? The employees. [Management] should cut back on company expenditures. The president of the company said that the economy was bad but CUNA Mutual had a better year this year than last!! The new personnel manager is working on how best to present an image of 'a sincere desire to do our best for our employees and bullshit them at the same time' while they take away but always smooth it over so it looks good."

The union democratization movement helped to pave the way for the formation in 1981 of the Women's Association by several women active in the union reform movement. Ostensibly, the association represented all women at the company—managerial, professional, and clerical employees—but the leaders were managers and professionals, and a bias toward their concerns was reflected in the stated purposes of the organization: to educate women in management skills, to encourage career development, and to identify opportunities for advancement. A statement in the first issue of *Woman to Woman*, the association's newsletter, expressed concern that office workers not be excluded: "I think we should try to reach not just the women in management but the clerical staff too."[8]

The Women's Association made efforts to address the broad concerns of all women at the company. *Woman to Woman* published articles on work-family conflict, career planning, and sex segregation in the workplace. It featured articles on the stress and low pay in clerical jobs and invited women to submit articles about their work experience. "I was a waitress during high school and liked the contact with people," wrote one clerical worker. "No matter what service you're offering, there is pride in having a satisfied customer."[9]

The Women's Association promoted a feminist agenda. Feminists were invited to speak on topics such as equal rights, sexual harassment, and comparable worth. And two of the goals of the Women's Association were to increase female participation in top management and institute pay equity. To this end, the association proposed that at least one woman be included on all management committees concerned with budgetary and policy decisions, that a women's advisory board be formed to address the promotion of women into higher-level management positions, and that a comparable-worth system be instituted to redress past sex discrimination.

Although its agenda was bold, the approach of the Women's Association was moderate. Leaders emphasized the importance of pursuing the association's goals in a "professional" manner. "We do not want management to see the Women's Association as just a bunch of angry women instead of listening to [us] and responding to what we say," one leader explained. "We need to learn the corporate game, set up strategy, and move slowly but assertively."

The company responded favorably to the Women's Association and granted women access to company resources and permission to hold meetings on company time. Management also anticipated the women's agenda. This was most evident in the company's decision to conduct a job evaluation study to preempt the women's demands for pay equity.[10] "We want to be able to talk about the comparability in terms of pay in other companies," reported one top-level manager.

> We are proposing a plan that . . . takes factor rating points and assigns [the job] to a category. . . . We are consciously trying to correct these inequities because of the nuisance value of the comparable-worth issue. We are trying to anticipate that these initiatives could come from the women employees. We try to maintain a good, viable employee-relations environment. . . . Pretty soon, [the Women's Association] will make demands. They have raised the comparable-worth issue but it is safe to say that we are one step ahead of them.

It would be premature to predict the likely impact of the new union structure and the Women's Association on company policies. However, it appears unlikely that either organization will offer a militant challenge to managerial control at CUNA Mutual. The company's openness toward both initiatives helped to shape the approaches of the union and the Women's Association. Management did not stand in the way of the democratization movement even though it weakened management's control over the union. Nor did the company discourage the formation of the Women's Association even though it led to proposals that might be costly. Because the company created a climate conducive to these employee initiatives, the union and the Women's Association proceeded with moderation.

124

Conclusion

The work experience and strategies of employees at the CUNA Mutual Insurance Society demonstrate the contradictory impact of a human-relations managerial approach on collective activism. In its early years, the company was successful in creating a partnership—an identity of interests—between management and union employees. As long as the company provided superior wages, benefits, and working conditions to its workers, the union's role as an extension of management went unquestioned. This arrangement began to break down when the automation and reorganization of work led to a partial erosion of the favorable conditions that had guaranteed employee loyalty to the firm. Management then turned to participatory policies, hoping to increase productivity and job satisfaction at the same time.

Participatory management offered a partial substitute for corporate benevolence. Where workers' suggestions led to new policies that improved their working conditions, increased satisfaction resulted. But where workers' recommendations were ignored, new frustrations emerged. A contradiction was built into the quality circle program from the start: As a top-down management initiative, the quality circle program invited employees to participate but limits were placed on the parameters of their participation. Hence, participatory management sometimes backfired, raising employee expectations beyond what management had intended.

The shift to participatory management helped to lay the basis for the democratization of the union and the formation of the Women's Association. The democratization movement loosened the symbiotic ties between management and union and more sharply delineated the interests of the two groups. The Women's Association challenged the sexism at the company reflected in the low pay of women's jobs and the exclusion of women from middle and top management jobs. Only time will tell what the long-term impact of these employee initiatives will be, but their initial actions suggest that both the union and the Women's Association will pursue moderation rather than militance.

The absence of militance at CUNA Mutual was not surprising given the culture of the workplace and its superior working conditions. The human-relations managerial philosophy shaped employees' strategies as well as management's. Both groups were committed to negotiating within the rules. More important, the persistence of favorable working conditions gave the workers and their organizations an objective reason to identify with the firm. Despite the erosion in promotional opportunities, wages and benefits were better at CUNA Mutual than at other insurance companies in town. For women at the company, their exclusion from top management was a sore point, but their access to supervisory and middle-management positions offered greater opportunities than were available elsewhere. And despite the limited nature of the employee participation program at CUNA Mutual, employees enjoyed greater autonomy than is typical in insurance firms. Not only did these factors make a real difference in the day-to-day work lives of employees at CUNA Mutual, but they also shaped workers' assessment of whether they'd get a better deal if they left.

Management-labor relations at CUNA Mutual looked very different from the Trust and WPS, where insensitive and authoritarian management policies provoked extensive dissatisfaction. At these other two insurance companies, collective grievances did not automatically lead to collective action. It was only when conditions were right—when the work setting allowed it, when union resources were accessible, and when the threat of managerial repression was not prohibitive—that the office workers at the Trust and WPS were able to organize.

At CUNA Mutual, the first precondition for collective action—objectionable managerial practices that polarize management and workers—was missing. The work setting and employee organizations allowed ample opportunities to communicate shared grievances with little fear of management retaliation. But management's policies did not provoke the type of dissatisfaction that leads to the development of oppositional networks. The bottom line at CUNA Mutual was that management's philosophy and policies created an atmosphere more conducive to cooperation than conflict. Grievances, even collective grievances, did emerge, but these grievances were readily accommodated within the mechanisms developed by management and the employee organizations to resolve conflicts.

From one angle, this case demonstrates the effectiveness of the human-relations managerial style in containing and co-opting workers' actions. It shows that the carrot is more effective than the stick: As long as a company provides positive rewards instead of negative sanctions, employees are unlikely to challenge managerial authority. At the same time, however, this case underscores the somewhat delicate balancing act that a company must maintain to integrate workers into a structure that management essentially controls. Workers only positively identify with their employer so long as real benefits and incentives are provided. If changes in the company's position prompt management to withdraw these enticements, employee dissatisfaction will likely increase, as will the potential for a collective challenge.

NOTES

1. The data for chapter 5 were derived from nine semistructured interviews with managers at CUNA Mutual and twelve semistructured interviews with employees at CUNA Mutual. The interviews with office workers addressed work history, family status, work experiences at CUNA Mutual, and participation in the union and Women's Association. The interviews with managers covered the history of CUNA Mutual, the company philosophy, managerial policies and responsibilities, and management-union relations. The interviews have been slightly edited for grammar and punctuation. Additional materials—company pamphlets, newsletters, and labor contracts—were provided by CUNA Mutual and by Local 39 of the Office and Professional Employees International Union.

2. Charles Eikel, *The Debt Shall Die with the Debtor: The CUNA Mutual Insurance Story* (New York: Newcomen Society in North America, 1972).

3. The influence of Filene on CUNA Mutual was ideological as well as financial. Describing CUNA Mutual's decision to hold open area meetings among policyholders, Charles F. Eikel, in *The Debt Shall Die with the Debtor*, states, "It was pure democracy reminiscent of the old town meetings. Like Filene wanting to give his customers a fair dollar's worth, we genuinely want to hear from our policyowners," 31.

4. CUNA Mutual had 600 additional employees—a field force of 250–300 employees and 300 workers—in the California branch of the company.

5. See Barbara Baran and Suzanne Teegarden, "Women's Labor in the Insurance Office," Department of City and Regional Planning, University of California, Berkeley, 1983, Mimeo.

6. CUNA Mutual executives considered a variety of approaches for increasing productivity, including the use of time and motion studies as the basis for tightening productivity standards. Due to negative experiences with a time and motion study in the fifties, management was not interested in alienating its workers. See Dick Glimerveen, Rob Henning, and John Taylor, "Case Study: Quality Commitment at CUNA Mutual," Industrial Engineering Department, University of Wisconsin-Madison, 1982, Mimeo.

7. Ibid.

8. *Woman to Woman*, vol. 1, no. 1, Mar. 1981.

9. *Woman to Woman*, vol. 3, no. 1, Feb. 1983.

10. See Heidi I. Hartmann, ed. *Comparable Worth: New Directions for Research* (Washington, D.C.: National Academy Press, 1985).

6

Conclusion

We're Worth It! challenges traditional views of working women's passivity and demonstrates that office workers are actors who forge their own responses to work and family. The strike at the Wisconsin Education Association Insurance Trust and the unionization drive at the Wisconsin Physicians Services Insurance Corporation (WPS) offered the most dramatic examples of clerical activism. But even the homeworkers circumvented company policies by setting their own work pace and by consulting with each other, while office workers at the CUNA Mutual Insurance Society asserted their autonomy by democratizing the union and forming the Women's Association. While often partial and incomplete, these initiatives nevertheless attested to the resourcefulness and resilience of office workers on the job.

This study of office workers in the insurance industry joins other research on women hospital workers, sales clerks, and factory workers in offering an important corrective to the stereotype about working women's passivity.[1] At the same time, the evidence presented here warns against drawing simple conclusions about working women's activism. The experience of these office workers reinforces the need for careful examination of the structural conditions that encourage women's activism and those that impede it.[2]

In each of the four cases, managerial practices and styles together with characteristics of the work setting and access to resources were crucial factors shaping women's organizing efforts. Specifically, these office workers mobilized for collective action when managerial practices provided them

129

with a clear target for their grievances, when the threat of managerial repression was not prohibitive, when the structure of work provided opportunities to develop ties of solidarity, and when women had access to resources, especially union resources, that encouraged their activism.[3]

At the Trust, all four conditions were present prior to the strike. Patriarchal and authoritarian managerial practices provoked extensive grievances when already problematic conditions deteriorated. The structural relationship between the Trust and the state teachers' union placed constraints on Trust management that protected office workers from management repression. The centralization of office workers in one building encouraged the development of communication networks and ties of solidarity at work. And the division of the labor union into three bargaining units provided the women with the opportunity to control their own labor organization. It was within this context that the women developed the necessary ties of solidarity, both at work and within their labor union, to initiate a strike.

At WPS, authoritarian managerial practices and a deterioration in working conditions prompted the initial unionization drive. After unionization, the persistence of coercive managerial practices continued to provoke employee grievances, but other factors discouraged collective activism. The separation of office workers across several office buildings blocked communication among union workers. The threat of management repression impeded the development of social ties at work and made workers fear they would jeopardize their jobs should they go on strike. The union's continuing struggle with WPS management just to maintain the status quo contributed to the estrangement of the rank and file and made collective mobilization difficult.

The arbitrary practices of WPS management catalyzed grievances among WPS homeworkers as well. However, the decentralized structure of homework inhibited the development of the broad social ties necessary for collective action. In addition, the threat of repression discouraged activism among the WPS homeworkers who felt vulnerable to management retaliation. Although the union representing the WPS work force attempted to organize the homeworkers, the women's isolation and family commitments reinforced their low level of interest in unionization. In the absence of union representation, the homeworkers' initiatives were limited to individual strategies and an occasional collective expression of discontent.

In sharp contrast to the other two firms, the benevolent and participatory practices of CUNA Mutual created a relatively satisfied work force. Although employees complained about specific issues, pervasive grievances never emerged. Office workers had ample opportunities to develop social networks and initiate changes at work and within their employee organizations, but they had little motivation to transform those ties into oppositional networks. The democratization movement made the union more responsive to office workers' concerns, and the Women's Association provided a vehicle for articulating women's interests, but moderation characterized the approach of both organizations.

When office workers are in circumstances that provide them with a strong reason as well as the capacity to act collectively, they do act, but have a variety of courses to choose from. The strike at the Trust illustrates that collective action results only from extreme conditions. Strikes are highly unusual and dramatic events that require working women to step outside their everyday circumstances and take significant risks—risks of management retaliation and risks of disrupting family life. Hence, strikes are unlikely unless grievances accumulate to the point where women conclude that they have no recourse—that every alternative with management has been exhausted. The decision to strike must be collective, and to develop the collective consciousness necessary to initiate a strike, the work setting and labor union must provide opportunities to communicate shared grievances. Strikes also require a collective assessment that the benefits to be gained from collective action outweigh the risks. Here, the Trust situation was unusual: The structural ties to the state teachers' union reduced the risks of striking. For strikes to occur in other insurance settings, unions must find alternative avenues for exerting pressure on management.

The WPS case underscores the obstacles to collective action posed by authoritarian managerial policies. Following unionization at WPS, authoritarian management practices created pervasive dissatisfaction, but these conditions also produced a vulnerable and fragmented work force.[4] In situations like WPS, the challenge for a labor union is significant. Because managerial surveillance impedes the development of ties of solidarity at work, these ties must be developed outside of work. Lacking alternatives, working women are likely to bite the bullet and, whenever possible, quit.[5]

A comparision of the Trust and WPS points to the different conditions that promote unionization and strikes. Both forms of activism require deep dissatisfaction with the current employment conditions and a perception that collective action could be instrumental in improving these conditions. And with both unionization and strikes, a crucial issue is whether the company's powers of intimidation prove stronger than the workers' desire for better conditions.[6] But there is one crucial difference between unionization and strikes: The decision to strike requires greater risks of the individual than the decision to unionize. To join a union, employees privately vote for union certification in an election. Of course, the risks are not insignificant—management's harassment of known union supporters often discourages workers from voting for a union. But the stakes are higher during a strike: As a highly visible action, strikes make workers especially vulnerable to management retaliation. This is part of the reason that strikes are less common than unionization drives. Although the two forms of collective action have common causes, grievances must be more acute to compensate for the greater risks taken during a strike.

The WPS homework case underscores the limitations to women's activism in isolated work settings. That these women did forge social networks indicates that in almost any work setting women will develop social ties and friendships as an outlet for work-based grievances and a source of advice for how to deal with management. But social networks and collective action are not the same thing. For women to engage in collective action, a common consciousness about their working conditions must emerge. For this, women need opportunities—either at work or in a labor organization—to develop broad social networks. The isolation of homeworkers diminishes the communication possibilities at work and reduces women's access to labor resources as well.[7]

The CUNA Mutual case demonstrates the limited nature of collective activism in workplaces with a human-relations management style. As long as a company provides its workers with better conditions than its competitors—whether through wages and benefits, promotions and training opportunities, or participatory programs—workers have less motivation to challenge managerial control. The human-relations approach is not foolproof, however. As a top-down strategy for simultaneously meeting productivity goals and organizing employee commitment to the firm, the human-relations management style sometimes backfires: If management choses productivity over employee satisfaction workers may become alienated and respond with initiatives of their own. However, these initiatives are likely to take the form of moderate efforts to increase employees' leverage with management rather than militant forms of collective action.

The evidence from these cases demonstrates that the consciousness of working women is in a state of flux. This was especially apparent with the women at the Trust and the WPS homeworkers. At the Trust, management's reference to the employees as "secondary wage earners" contradicted women's emerging identification of themselves as workers. At the same time, the company's inflexibility undercut women's ability to respond to family commitments and crises. Thus, it was the combination of women's work- and family-based identities that underwrote their demands for respect and equality in the workplace. The feminist consciousness born of the strike, in turn, reverberated on women's post-strike behavior as they became more willing to assert their rights in the workplace and at home.

Unlike the women at the Trust, many of the homeworkers accepted their status as secondary wage earners—at least while their children were young. Homework represented a strategy for fulfilling women's traditional responsibilities at home while also preserving their ties to the labor market. In this sense, traditional values underpinned homeworkers' "choice" of a marginal work situation. Yet, these women were not unaffected by the women's movement. Echoes of the feminist call for respect on the job were heard in home-workers'complaints about their working conditions.

These cases illustrate how feminist and traditional values coexist in an uneasy balance in the consciousness of today's working women. Few women have escaped the influence of the women's movement—even those who, like the home-workers, would distance themselves from feminist styles and principles. Widely held by working women is the feminist view that women deserve respect and equal opportunity in the workplace. At the same time, however, women's family commitments often shape their consciousness and strategies at work.[8]

Many working women find themselves caught between an older notion of themselves as homemakers and mothers and a newer notion of themselves as workers with certain rights on the job and in the home. Whether the precarious balance that exists between these two notions comes unhinged depends upon women's particular household and work experiences. In the case of the homeworkers, women's household responsibilities limited their ability to build social networks and develop a critical consciousness. In the case of the Trust, women's form of employment, particularly full-time employment in a centralized work setting, lessened their family ties and encouraged the development of sufficient solidarity to engage in collective action.[9]

Of course, collective action requires more than work settings that promote social interaction. Pervasive dissatisfactions with working conditions must also exist. Today, office automation is affecting women's job satisfaction. At the Trust, the influence of the union, together with the small size of the firm, tempered the effects of office automation. The labor contract resulting from the strike prevented management from introducing individualized productivity expectancies (at least in the first three years following the strike). In addition, the small size of the firm required the creation of specialized, quasi-professional jobs. The introduction of new jobs requiring a higher level of skill partially substituted for the jobs that were deskilled by the introduction of computers. Objections to speedups and the downgrading of certain adjusting jobs were voiced, but collective dissatisfaction with automation was not evident.

At both WPS and CUNA Mutual, the larger size of the companies led to greater subdivision of tasks. The different philosophies of the two firms, however, affected the way office automation proceded. At WPS, individualized productivity expectancies were established for each job, and negative sanctions followed for those office workers unable to meet the expectancies. Equally affected were those employees who worked with computers and those who did not. The union did contest management's most grievous abuses of the rate-expectancy system, but this had only limited impact on the majority of office workers. The union could offer no protections to the WPS homeworkers. For those WPS employees consigned to the most routine and repetitive jobs, the tyranny of Taylorism was all too apparent. Grievances with the rate-expectancy system were widespread, but the focus of employee discontent was management coercion, rather than computer technology.

By contrast, the effects of office automation were softened by the benevolent managerial style at CUNA Mutual. Productivity expectancies were associated with most of the computer-based clerical jobs, but work teams and quality circles gave workers some input into the work process. This led to changes that increased the variety and mobility in some departments. Office workers' exclusion from corporate decisions regarding new computer systems did cause some dissatisfaction, but there was little evidence of pervasive dissatisfaction with office automation at CUNA Mutual.

That the office workers' experience of office automation was not uniform across or even within work settings confirms other research. Studies show that office workers often enjoy working with computers but object to certain managerial practices—such as productivity expectancies and computer monitoring.[10] For automation to become the focus of organizing, office workers must conclude that the way management is deploying new technologies is unfair. Where clerical workers are subject to rigid productivity quotas and speedups, office automation can contribute to significant dissatisfaction, but where women are given the chance to learn new skills on the job, office automation can enhance their satisfaction with work.

The most important factor shaping office workers' job satisfaction in these workplaces was the managerial style. The patriarchal style at the prestrike Trust and WPS is probably a bit dated. Office workers still encounter sexual harassment, sexist attitudes, and sex discrimination in hiring and promotion practices that continue to generate dissatisfaction among office workers whose expectations have been raised by the women's movement. But sexism in the office workplace is often more subtle now, manifested in pay inequities, discriminatory benefits policies, and women's exclusion from middle- and top-level management positions.

There is some evidence that the insurance industry is beginning to turn away from authoritarian practices of the type found at WPS. At the least, authoritarian management generates employee dissatisfaction; at the most, it leads to employee activism. Many insurance corporations are interested in avoiding both. Industry journals report that office workers are increasingly unwilling to accept abusive treatment: "Take the matter of discipline, which traditionally was the province of supervision. Subordinates expected to be disciplined for offenses. Punishment was accepted, even if it was too harsh or unfairly distributed. Today's employees want to know what specific discipline to expect (or lack of it). . . . It is increasingly difficult to discipline employees in an arbitrary and capricious manner and get away with it."[11] To avoid unionization, industry analysts urge insurance executives to replace "authoritarian" managerial styles with "participatory management." "Unless insurance companies want to fall in the same situation as many manufacturing companies . . . with their ironclad union contracts and work rules," one commentator urged, "a system of upward communication is a vital necessity. Only such a 'listen to the employee' system can tell management on a continuing basis from month to month what employees really think and feel about their work situation and their employers. . . . Listening to employees also is a way for employers to invite employees to participate in decisions affecting their operations, procedures, and jobs—and at the same time forestall union organizers."[12]

The insurance industry is experimenting with participatory management—through quality circles, job enrichment programs, and work teams.[13] Participatory management is generally limited to those larger organizations with reputations for innovative practices, such as CUNA Mutual. Hence, only a minority of office workers have gained experience with participatory management. In those companies where quality circles have been introduced, employees' decision-making responsibility typically remains relatively limited.[14]

The insurance industry has been on the forefront of a trend that threatens to remove women even further from the possibilty of influencing corporate decision making—the growth of the contingent workforce. The contingent workforce includes part-time, temporary, and home-based workers. The majority of contingent workers are employed by service-sector firms—insurance companies, banks, fast-food restaurants, and retail establishments. Part-time jobs now constitute more than one-fifth of all U.S. employment; six million Americans are presently working in part-time jobs. And the temporary services industry, which includes companies such as Kelley Services, is the third-fastest growing industry in the economy.[15] The data on home-based workers is more difficult to collect since many homeworkers are part of the underground economy. Nevertheless, the Bureau of Labor Statistics reported that in 1985, 246,000 people worked eight hours or more a week as home-based secretaries, stenographers, and typists.[16]

From a management perspective, the hiring of contingent workers provides cost savings and flexibility. Instead of hiring full-time employees at competitive wages and benefits, employers hire contingent workers and save on both. By making only a limited commitment to contingent workers, employers' flexibility is enhanced since the size of the work force can be increased or decreased in response to fluctuations in the company's competitive position. Part-time, temporary, and home-based workers are also less likely to organize into unions. Their weaker attachment to the firm, together with their isolation in the case of home-based workers, pose significant barriers to unionization.

The growth of contingent work arrangements, in the insurance industry and elsewhere, has problematic consequences for working women. This was clearly evident at WPS where the part-time, temporary, and home-based workers received no benefits and lower wages than their full-time counterparts. Nor did these workers have the limited union protections provided to the full-time workers. As long as women retain primary responsibility for the household and child care, they will seek work arrangements that allow them to juggle their wage-earning and family needs. But the impetus for the growth of part-time, temporary, and home-based work is not coming primarily from women but rather from employers seeking a source of marginal labor to increase their profits and flexibility. Many of the women in part-time and temporary jobs would prefer to work full-time but are unable to find full-time employment.

Finally, these cases reveal the obstacles to women's organizing in the absence of a working women's movement. Though organizations like 9 to 5: The National Association of Working Women have successfully conducted public-education campaigns on issues such as contingent work, office automation, and pay equity that have increased expectations among office workers, there has been no significant surge in activism among office workers here and elsewhere.

138

Conclusion

The women at the Trust framed their strike demands in terms of "working women's rights." In so doing, they drew on a long tradition within the labor movement of organizing for workers' rights, as well as the demand of the recent women's movement for women's rights in both the public and private arenas.[17] In actuality, however, their definition of *rights* was simply women's "right" to respect and decent treatment on the job. Following the strike, the changes initiated by management—office automation, limited participatory processes, and greater promotional opportunities—caught the union women off-guard. Had the women at the Trust been part of a larger self-conscious movement, they might have channeled the knowledge gained from the strike into new arenas, pushing for greater influence over the technological and organizational changes taking place at work.

A working women's movement would combine the best of the women's movement and the labor movement into organizations that could promote a working women's agenda. For the labor movement, this could help to reverse the decades-long decline in trade-union membership. Since the mid-fifties, the percentage of the unionized workforce has been steadily declining from a peak of approximately 35 percent of the nonagricultural labor force to approximately 17 percent today.[18] The growing and dynamic service sectors of the economy are today largely unorganized. Women workers—who make up most of the labor force in the service sector—are interested in unionization.[19] This is not surprising, given that the major impact of unions is to improve the wages, benefits, and working conditions of lower-wage, lower-skill workers who lack individual labor market power and mobility. The majority of women in the labor force work in low-wage jobs and would greatly benefit from unionization.

In recent years, the labor movement has started to focus its attention on organizing service-sector workers. In two important reports by the AFL-CIO Committee on the Evolution of Work, "The Future of Work" and "The Changing Situation of Workers and Their Unions," labor leaders called for an aggressive organizing campaign aimed at the service sector.[20]

But labor unions must do more than commit their resources to organizing working women. If unions are to fully realize their potential as representatives of women workers, they must incorporate women into leadership positions and women's concerns into the union's goals. Women workers have unsatisfied demands in such areas as pay equity, career development, child care, and maternity leave. The challenge for unions is to provide leadership in these new domains and to link women's rights to the still important pay and employment security concerns felt by women workers.

On the job, at the bargaining table, and sometimes on the picket line, office workers are beginning to assert their common interests as working women. It is partially because feminists have validated women's right to respectful treatment on the job that working women are developing a consciousness of their rights on the job. This consciousness is underwriting women's claims for equality and, in some cases, providing the first step toward a broader consciousness of power relations in the workplace. The development of a more general critique is by no means automatic, however. Yes, women need equal treatment and respect on the job, but they also need equal pay, equal representation at all levels of management, flexible policies supportive of family commitments, and, perhaps most important, a real voice in the organizational and technological decisions that shape women's work lives. By linking proposals for working women's rights to broader issues of control at work, the full potential of a working women's agenda could be realized.

NOTES

1. See Barbara Melosh, *The Physician's Hand: Work Culture and Conflict in American Nursing* (Philadelphia: Temple University Press, 1982); Karen Brodkin Sacks, *Caring by the Hour: Women, Work, and Organizing at Duke Medical Center* (Urbana: University of Illinois Press, 1988); Susan Porter Benson, *Counter Cultures: Saleswomen, Managers, and Customers in American Department Stores, 1890–1940* (Urbana: University of Illinois Press, 1986); and Nina

Shapiro-Perl, "The Piece Rate: Class Struggle on the Shop Floor. Evidence from the Costume Jewelry Industry in Providence, Rhode Island," in *Case Studies on the Labor Process*, ed. Andrew Zimbalist (New York: Monthly Review Press, 1979), 277–98.

2. In the introduction to her edited collection, *Women, Work, and Protest: A Century of U.S. Women's Labor History* (Boston: Routledge and Kegan Paul, 1985), Ruth Milkman argues that in challenging the old orthodoxy about working women's passivity, the new feminist scholarship has made an important contribution. Milkman argues that feminist scholarship has a tendency to paint a picture of an inexhaustible reservoir of female militancy. As the mirror image of the old, this new perspective fails to specify the structural opportunities for protest or to acknowledge any constraints on women's organizing efforts.

3. These conclusions build on the important work of Louise A. Tilly, "Paths of Proletarianization: Organization of Production, Sexual Division of Labor, and Women's Collective Action," *Signs* 10 (Winter 1981): 400–417.

4. See Evelyn Nakano Glenn and Roslyn L. Feldberg, "Proletarianizing Clerical Work: Technology and Organizational Control in the Office," in *Case Studies on the Labor Process*, ed. Zimbalist, 242–56.

5. Daniel B. Cornfield, "Economic Segmentation and Expression of Labor Unrest: Striking Versus Quitting in the Manufacturing Sector," Department of Sociology, Vanderbelt University, June 1983, Mimeo.

6. Richard Edwards, *Contested Terrain: The Transformation of the Workplace in the Twentieth Century* (New York: Basic Books, 1979).

7. For other sources on the social context of home-based work, see Kathleen Christensen, ed., *The New Era of Home-based Work: Directions and Policies* (Boulder: Westview, 1988), and Eileen Boris and Cynthia R. Daniels, eds., *Homework: Historical and Contemporary Perspectives on Paid Labor at Home* (Urbana: University of Illinois Press, 1989).

8. Several recent collections focus on the sources of women's consciousness and activism. See Milkman, ed., *Women, Work, and Protest*; Carol Groneman and Mary Beth Norton, eds., *"To Toil the Livelong Day": America's Women at Work, 1780–1980* (Ithaca: Cornell University Press, 1987); Ann Bookman and Sandra Morgen, eds., *Women and the Politics of Empowerment* (Philadelphia: Temple University Press, 1988); and Karen Brodkin Sacks and Dorothy Remy, eds., *My Troubles Are Going to Have Trouble with Me: Everyday Trials and Triumphs of Women Workers* (New Brunswick, N.J.: Rutgers University Press, 1984).

9. Louise A. Tilly, in "Paths of Proletarianization," drew similar

conclusions about the variable impact of the household division of labor on women's activism. Tilly's study of nineteenth-century French women in the cotton, textile, and tobacco industries demonstrated that the household division of labor was a crucial factor in determining women's participation in collective action. It was only in the cases where women's lifetime commitments to one job lessened their familial ties that women were able to develop sufficient solidarity to engage in collective action.

10. See Heidi I. Hartmann, Robert E. Kraut, and Louise A. Tilly, eds., *Computer Chips and Paper Clips: Technology and Women's Employment, Volume I* (Washington, D.C.: National Academy Press, 1986) for a synthesis of this research.

11. Mathew Goodfellow, "Avoiding Unions in the Insurance Clerical Field," *Best's Review Property/Casualty Edition* 81 (1980): 118.

12. Ibid.

13. David Armstrong and Christine Nuttal, "Managing the Efficient Automated Workplace," *Best's Review Life/Health Edition* 82 (1981): 48–56.

14. Thomas A. Kochan, Harry C. Katz, and Robert B. McKersie, eds., *The Transformation of American Industrial Relations* (New York: Basic Books, 1986); Charlotte Gold, *Labor-Management Committees: Confrontation, Cooptation, or Cooperation* (Ithaca: ILR Press, 1986); and Tom Juravich, *Chaos on the Shop Floor: A Worker's View of Quality, Productivity, and Management* (Philadelphia: Temple University Press, 1985).

15. Bureau of National Affairs, *The Changing Workplace: New Directions in Staffing and Scheduling* (Washington, D.C.: Bureau of National Affairs, 1986).

16. Fran Horvath, "Work at Home: New Findings from the Current Population Survey," *Monthly Labor Review* 109 (Nov. 1986): 31–35.

17. See Gertrude Ezorsky, ed., *Moral Rights in the Workplace* (Albany: State University of New York Press, 1987); Alice Kessler-Harris, *Out to Work: A History of Wage-earning Women in the United States* (New York: Oxford University Press, 1982); Groneman and Norton, eds., *"To Toil the Livelong Day"*; and Bookman and Morgen, eds., *Women and the Politics of Empowerment*.

18. U.S. Department of Labor Bureau of Labor Statistics, *Employment and Earnings*, vol. 37, Jan. 1990 (Washington, D.C.: U.S. Department of Labor, 1990).

19. Kochan, Katz, and McKersie, eds., *The Transformation*, 217.

20. AFL-CIO Committee on the Evolution of Work, "The Changing Situation of Workers and Their Unions," Feb. 1985, and "The Future of Work," Aug. 1983.

Bibliography

Acker, Joan, and Donald Van Houten. 1974. "Differential Recruitment and Control: The Sex Structuring of Organizations." *Administrative Science Quarterly* 19:152–62.

AFL-CIO Committee on the Evolution of Work. 1985. "The Changing Situation of Workers and Their Unions."

———. 1983. "The Future of Work."

Applebaum, Eileen. 1987. "Technology and the Redesign of Work in the Insurance Industry." In *Women, Work, and Technology: Transformations*, ed. Barbara Drygulski Wright. Ann Arbor: University of Michigan Press.

Armstrong, David, and Christine Nuttal. 1981. "Managing the Efficient Automated Workplace." *Best's Review Life/Health Edition* 82:48–56.

Aron, Cindy. 1981. "'To Barter Their Souls for Gold': Female Clerks in Federal Government Offices, 1862–1890." *Journal of American History* 67:835–53.

Balser, Diane. 1987. *Sisterhood and Solidarity: Feminism and Labor in Modern Times*. Boston: South End Press.

Baran, Barbara. 1987. "The Technological Transformation of White-Collar Work: A Case Study of the Insurance Industry." In *Computer Chips and Paper Clips: Case Studies and Policy Perspectives, Volume II*, ed. Heidi I. Hartmann. Washington, D.C.: National Academy Press.

Baran, Barbara, and Suzanne Teegarden. 1983. "Women's Labor in the Insurance Office." Department of City and Regional Planning, University of California, Berkeley. Mimeo.

Beechey, Veronica. 1978. "Women and Production: A Critical Analysis of Some Sociological Theories of Women's Work." In *Feminism and Materialism*, ed. Annette Kuhn and Anne Marie Wolpe. London: Routledge and Kegan Paul.

Benson, Susan Porter. 1986. *Counter Cultures: Saleswomen, Man-

agers, and Customers in American Department Stores, 1890–1940. Urbana: University of Illinois Press.

Bookman, Ann, and Sandra Morgen, eds. 1988. *Women and the Politics of Empowerment*. Philadelphia: Temple University Press.

Boris, Eileen, and Cynthia R. Daniels, eds. 1989. *Homework: Historical and Contemporary Perspectives on Paid Labor at Home*. Urbana: University of Illinois Press.

Braverman, Harry. 1974. *Labor and Monopoly Capital*. New York: Monthly Review Press.

Burawoy, Michael. 1979. *Manufacturing Consent: Changes in the Labor Process under Monopoly Capitalism*. Chicago: University of Chicago Press.

Bureau of National Affairs. 1986. *The Changing Workplace: New Directions in Staffing and Scheduling*. Washington, D.C.: Bureau of National Affairs.

Cameron, Ardis. 1985. "Bread and Roses Revisited: Women's Culture and Working-Class Activism in the Lawrence Strike of 1912." In *Women, Work and Protest: A Century of U.S. Women's Labor History*, Ruth Milkman, ed. Boston: Routledge and Kegan Paul.

Carter, Valerie. 1987. "Office Technology and Relations of Control in Clerical Work Organization." In *Women, Work, and Technology: Transformations*, ed. Barbara Drygulski Wright. Ann Arbor: University of Michigan Press.

Center for the Study of Organizational Productivity, Graduate School of Business, University of Wisconsin. 1985. "WEA Insurance Trust: Organizational Survey, Feedback Report."

Christensen, Kathleen. 1988. *Women and Home-based Work: The Unspoken Contract*. New York: Henry Holt.

———, ed. 1988. *The New Era of Home-based Work: Directions and Policies*. Boulder: Westview.

Cornfield, Daniel B. 1983. "Economic Segmentation and Expression of Labor Unrest: Striking Versus Quitting in the Manufacturing Sector." Department of Sociology, Vanderbilt University. Mimeo.

Costello, Cynthia B. 1987. *Home-based Employment: Implications for Working Women*. Washington, D.C.: Women's Research and Education Institute.

Czyson, Janice. 1982. "Long Skirts Prompt Legal Battle," *The Feminist Connection*, Dec. 1982.

Bibliography

Davies, Margery. 1982. *Woman's Place Is at the Typewriter: Office Work and Office Workers, 1870–1930*. Philadelphia: Temple University Press.

de Kadt, Maarten. 1979. "Insurance: A Clerical Work Factory?" in *Case Studies on the Labor Process*, ed. Andrew Zimbalist. New York: Monthly Review Press.

Dublin, Thomas. 1979. *Women at Work: The Transformation of Work and Community in Lowell, Massachusetts, 1820–1860*. New York: Columbia University Press.

Edwards, Richard. 1979. *Contested Terrain: The Transformation of the Workplace in the Twentieth Century*. New York: Basic Books.

Eikel, Charles. 1972. *The Debt Shall Die with the Debtor: The CUNA Mutual Insurance Story*. New York: Newcomen Society in North America.

Eisenstein, Sarah. 1983. *Give Us Bread but Give Us Roses*. Boston: Routledge and Kegan Paul.

Evans, Sara. 1979. *Personal Politics: The Roots of Women's Liberation in the Civil Rights Movement and the New Left*. New York: Alfred A. Knopf.

Ezorsky, Gertrude, ed. 1987. *Moral Rights in the Workplace*. Albany: State University of New York Press.

Feldberg, Roslyn L. 1980. "'Union Fever': Organizing among Clerical Workers, 1900–1930." *Radical America* 14:53–67.

Feldberg, Roslyn L., and Evelyn Nakano Glenn. 1983. "Technology and Work Degradation." In *Machina Ex Dea*, ed. Joan Rothchild. New York: Pergamon Press.

Ferree, Myra Marx. 1985. "Between Two Worlds: German Feminist Approaches to Working Class Women and Work." *Signs* 10:517–36.

Garson, Barbara. 1977. *All the Livelong Day: The Meaning and Demeaning of Routine Work*. New York: Penguin Books.

Glenn, Evelyn Nakano, and Roslyn L. Feldberg. 1979. "Proletarianizing Clerical Work: Technology and Organizational Control in the Office." In *Case Studies on the Labor Process*, ed. Andrew Zimbalist. New York: Monthly Review Press.

Glimerveen, Dick, Rob Henning, and John Taylor. 1982. "Case Study: Quality Commitment at CUNA Mutual." Industrial Engineering Department, University of Wisconsin-Madison. Mimeo.

Gold, Charlotte. 1986. *Labor-Management Committees: Confron-*

145

tation, Cooptation, or Cooperation. Ithaca: ILR Press.

Goldberg, Roberta. 1983. *Organizing Women Office Workers: Dissatisfaction, Consciousness, and Action*. New York: Praeger.

Goodfellow, Mathew. 1980. "Avoiding Unions in the Insurance Clerical Field." *Best's Review Property/Casualty Edition* 81: 118.

Gordon, Linda, and Allen Hunter. 1977–78. "Sex, Family, and the New Right: Anti-feminism as a Political Force." *Radical America* 11:1–17.

Gregory, Judith. 1982. "Technological Change in the Office Workplace and Implications for Organizing." In *Labor and Technology: Union Responses to Changing Environments*, ed. Donald Kennedy, Charles Craypo, and Mary Lehman. University Park: Pennsylvania State University Press.

Groneman, Carol, and Mary Beth Norton, eds. 1987. *"To Toil the Livelong Day": America's Women at Work, 1780–1980*. Ithaca: Cornell University Press.

Harrison, Cynthia. 1988. *On Account of Sex: The Politics of Women's Issues*. Berkeley: University of California Press.

Hartmann, Heidi I., ed. 1985. *Comparable Worth: New Directions for Research*. Washington, D.C.: National Academy Press.

Hartmann, Heidi I., Robert E. Kraut, and Louise A. Tilly, eds. 1986. *Computer Chips and Paper Clips: Technology and Women's Employment, Volume I*. Washington, D.C.: National Academy Press.

Herman, Andrew. 1982. "Conceptualizing Control: Domination and Hegemony in the Capitalist Labor Process." *Insurgent Sociologist* 11:7–22.

Hill, Ann. 1981. "District 925: A New Union for Office Workers?" *Socialist Review* 11:142–46

Horvath, Fran. 1986. "Work at Home: New Findings from the Current Population Survey." *Monthly Labor Review* 109: 31–35.

Hunt, Pauline. 1981. *Gender and Class Consciousness*. New York: Homes and Meier.

Juravich, Tom. 1985. *Chaos on the Shop Floor: A Worker's View of Quality, Productivity, and Management*. Philadelphia: Temple University Press.

Kanter, Rosabeth Moss. 1977. *Men and Women of the Corporation*. New York: Basic Books.

Kaplan, Temma. 1982. "Female Consciousness and Collective Action: The Case of Barcelona, 1910–1918." *Signs* 7:545–66.

Kennedy, Susan Estabrook. 1979. *If All We Did Was to Weep at Home: A History of White Working Class Women in America.* Bloomington: Indiana University Press.

Kessler-Harris, Alice. 1982. *Out to Work: A History of Wage-earning Women in the United States.* New York: Oxford University Press.

———. 1979. "Where Are the Organized Women Workers?" In *A Heritage of Our Own*, ed. Nancy F. Cott and Elizabeth H. Pleck. New York: Simon and Schuster.

Klare, Karl E. 1982. "Labor Law and Liberal Political Imagination." *Socialist Review* 12:45–73.

Kochan, Thomas A., Harry C. Katz, and Robert B. McKersie, eds. 1986. *The Transformation of American Industrial Relations.* New York: Basic Books.

Ladd-Taylor, Molly. 1985. "Women Workers and the Yale Strike." *Feminist Studies* 11:465–89.

Machung, Anne. 1984. "Word Processing: Forward for Business, Backward for Women." In *My Troubles Are Going to Have Trouble with Me: Everyday Trials and Triumphs of Women Workers*, ed. Karen Brodkin Sacks and Dorothy Remy. New Brunswick, N.J.: Rutgers University Press.

McKinnon, Catherine A. 1979. *Sexual Harassment of Working Women: A Case Study of Sex Discrimination.* New Haven: Yale University Press.

Melosh, Barbara. 1982. *The Physician's Hand: Work Culture and Conflict in American Nursing.* Philadelphia: Temple University Press.

Milkman, Ruth, ed. 1985. *Women, Work, and Protest: A Century of U.S. Women's Labor History.* Boston: Routledge and Kegan Paul.

Mills, C. Wright. 1951. *White Collar.* New York: Oxford University Press.

Murphree, Mary C. 1984. "Brave New Office: The Changing World of the Legal Secretary." In *My Troubles Are Going to Have Trouble with Me: Everyday Trials and Triumphs of Women Workers*, ed. Karen Brodkin Sacks and Dorothy Remy. New Brunswick, N.J.: Rutgers University Press.

Noble, David. 1979. "Social Choice in Machine Design: The Case of Automatically Controlled Machine Tools." In *Case Studies on the Labor Process*, ed. Andrew Zimbalist. New York: Monthly Review Press.

Plotke, David. 1980. "Interview with Karen Nussbaum: Women Clerical Workers and Trade Unionism." *Socialist Review* 10:151–59.

Pollert, Anna. 1981. *Girls, Wives, Factory Lives*. London: Macmillan.

Purcell, Kate. 1979. "Militancy and Acquiescence among Women Workers." In *Fit Work for Women*, ed. Sandra Burman. New York: St. Martin's Press.

Reskin, Barbara F., and Heidi I. Hartmann, eds., 1986. *Women's Work, Men's Work: Sex Segregation on the Job*. Washington, D.C.: National Academy Press.

Rotella, Elyce J. 1981. *From Home to Office: U.S. Women at Work, 1870–1930*. Ann Arbor: UMI Research Press.

Sacks, Karen Brodkin. 1988. *Caring by the Hour: Women, Work, and Organizing at Duke Medical Center*. Urbana: University of Illinois Press.

Sacks, Karen Brodkin, and Dorothy Remy, eds. 1984. *My Troubles Are Going to Have Trouble with Me: Everyday Trials and Triumphs of Women Workers*. New Brunswick, N.J.: Rutgers University Press.

Sansbury, Gail. 1980. "'Now, What's the Matter with You Girls?': Clerical Workers Organize," *Radical America* 14:67–76.

Shapiro-Perl, Nina. 1979. "The Piece Rate: Class Struggle on the Shop Floor. Evidence from the Costume Jewelry Industry in Providence, Rhode Island." In *Case Studies on the Labor Process*, ed. Andrew Zimbalist. New York: Monthly Review Press.

Smith, Dorothy. 1981. "Women and Trade Unions: The U.S. and British Experience." *Resources for Feminist Research* 10:53–59.

Strom, Sharon Hartman. 1985. "'We're No Kitty Foyles': Organizing Office Workers for the Congress of Industrial Organizations, 1937–50." In *Women, Work, and Protest: A Century of U.S. Women's Labor History*, ed. Ruth Milkman. Boston: Routledge and Kegan Paul.

———. 1983. "Challenging 'Woman's Place': Feminism, the Left, and Industrial Unionism in the 1930's." *Feminist Studies* 9:359–86.

Tax, Meredith. 1980. *The Rising of the Women*. New York: Monthly Review Press.

Tentler, Leslie Woodcock. 1979. *Wage-earning Women: Industrial Work and Family Life in the United States, 1900–1930*. New York: Oxford University Press.

Tepperman, Jean. 1976. *Not Servants, Not Machines: Office Workers Speak Out*. Boston: Beacon Press.

Tilly, Louise A. 1981. "Paths of Proletarianization: Organization of Production, Sexual Division of Labor, and Women's Collective Action." *Signs* 10:400–417.

Troy, Leo, and Neil Sheflin, 1985. *Members, Union Sourcebook: Membership, Structure, and Finance Directory*. West Orange, N.J.: Industrial Relations Data and Information Services.

U.S. Department of Labor, Bureau of Labor Statistics. 1990. *Employment and Earnings*. Vol. 37. Washington, D.C.: U.S. Department of Labor.

———. 1989. *Employment and Earnings*. Vol. 36. Washington, D.C.: U.S. Department of Labor.

———. 1988. *Employment and Earnings*. Vol. 35. Washington, D.C.: U.S. Department of Labor.

Wagner, David. 1979. "Clerical Workers: How 'Unorganizable' Are They?" *Labor Center Review* 2:20–50.

Index

Absenteeism, 3, 70, 122
Activism, conditions promoting,
  among women office workers: absence of severe repression, 4, 10, 59,
  84, 110, 125, 130–32; access to
  union resources, 4, 10–11, 59, 107,
  126, 130–31, 139–40; automation
  and, 2, 7–8, 10, 61, 134–36; central-
  zed work settings, 4, 9–10, 59, 74,
  83, 107, 126, 130, 132–33; objectionable management practices, 4,
  59–62, 110, 126–27, 129–30, 131,
  133, 134–37
Ajustors, claims, 19, 25, 30, 47; at the
  Trust, 50–51; at WPS, 67, 88–89.
  See also Claims process
Administrative Technical Services
  (AdTech), 76–77
AFL-CIO, 10, 139
Antifeminism, 6–7
As the Trust Turns, 25, 27–28, 29–30,
  31, 32, 60
Automation, office, 2, 10; at CUNA
  Mutual, 113–16, 135; effect of, on
  workplace activism, 7–8, 10, 52,
  134–36; at the Trust, 20, 50–53, 56,
  61, 134–35; at WPS, 65, 73, 134–35

Backgrounds of workers: educational,
  28, 91; family, 23, 90; labor-union,
  24, 59
Benefits: at CUNA Mutual, 109, 111;
  lack of, for homeworkers, 87, 138;
  at the Trust, 36; at WPS, 66, 68, 81

Centralized work settings: impor-
  tance of, to collective action, 9–10,
  64–65, 74, 83, 107; at the Trust, 21,
  24, 59, 130, 134
Citibank, 9
Claims process: at the Trust, 19, 20,
  50–53, 56, 61; at WPS, 65, 67, 88–
  89
Class consciousness, 6, 43
Class distinctions: at the Trust, 21–
  22, 43, 56–57; at WPS, 66–67
Coalition of Labor Union Women, 10
Collective action, conditions for. *See*
  Activism, conditions promoting,
  among women office workers
Comparable worth, 124
Computers, 7, 50, 69, 89, 115–16. *See
  also* Automation, office
Consciousness, office workers', 6, 57–
  58, 134; class, 6, 43; feminist, 44–
  45, 60, 123, 133–34, 140; at the
  Trust, 41–47, 133
Contingent workforce, 76–79, 137–
  38. *See also* Homeworkers, clerical
Contract negotiations: at CUNA Mu-
  tual, 122; at the Trust, 18, 21, 26–
  29, 31, 32, 40, 52, 53–55; at WPS,
  68, 74–76, 79, 80–81, 83, 87
Corporate liberalism, 110
Credit Union National Association
  (CUNA), 110–11. *See also* CUNA
  Mutual
Credit Unions, 110–11; relation of, to
  CUNA Mutual, 110–11, 112, 113.
  See also CUNA Mutual
CUNA Mutual (CUNA Mutual Insur
  ance Society), 3–4, 135; absence of
  militance at, 126–27, 131, 133;
  campaign to democratize, 121–22,

Index

CUNA Mutual (*continued*)
125, 131; efforts to increase productivity at, 113–20: expansion of, in 1960s and after, 113; human-relations management at, 3, 109, 125, 126–27, 133, 135; participatory policies at, 3, 109, 117–20, 125, 137; promotional opportunities at, 116–18, 126; relation of, to credit unions, 110–11, 112, 113; superior working conditions at, 110–13, 115–16, 125, 126, 131, 133; union at, 109, 112–13, 121, 125–26; Women's Association at, 109, 122–24, 125–26, 131

Deskilling, 51, 52–53, 135
Dress code, 80, 85

Educational backgrounds, 28
Eisenstein, Sarah, 6
Equal Rights Amendment, 10
Expectancies, productivity, 7, 114–15; at WPS, 67, 68–70, 72–73, 90, 98, 102, 135
Families: labor-union connections of, 24; relation of, to workplace militancy, 31, 36–37, 42; workers' role in their, 22–23, 36, 133–34. *See also* Homeworkers, clerical, family responsibilities of
Feminism, 44–45, 60, 123, 133–34, 140. *See also* Women's movement
Filene, Edward A., 110, 111, 123n3
Fonda, Jane, 39

Geography, workplace. *See* Centralized work settings, importance of, to collective action
Grievances, filing of, 49, 53, 74, 80, 82

Harassment of union activists: at the Trust, 47–49; at WPS, 65, 67, 70–71, 74, 79–80
Homeworkers, clerical, 3, 86–88; attitude of union employees toward, 78; barriers to collective action by, 87, 103–4, 106–7, 132–33; creation of social networks by, 4, 87, 99–

102, 105–6, 132–33; family responsibilities of, 88, 90, 91, 92–97, 99, 105, 134, 138; hiring of, as part of anti-union strategy, 9, 78–79, 81, 86, 87–88; irregular work flow experienced by, 88, 99; isolation of, 93, 100, 107, 132–33; job satisfaction and dissatisfaction of, 97–99, 100–103, 105, 134; limited contact of, with supervisors, 89–90; motivations of, 90–92, 93, 105; strategies of, 100–104; 106; tasks done by, 9–10, 88–89; and the union, 103–4, 130–31, 135; wages of, 87, 90, 91, 103
Husbands, 36–37, 42, 93–94, 96–97

Insurance industry, 4, 136–37. *See also* CUNA Mutual; Trust, the; WPS
Intimidation, 3, 47–48, 82; of homeworkers, 104; at WPS, 82, 83, 130–31, 132

Job-enrichment program, 119

Local 1401 (Retail Clerks union), 66–67, 73–74
Local 1444 (United Food and Commercial Workers), 74, 76, 77, 78–82, 103–4

Management styles: authoritarian, 2, 8; at the Trust, 21–24, 47, 58, 130; authoritarian, at WPS, 2–3, 65–66, 70–71, 79–80, 82, 84, 115, 130; human-relations, 8–9, 110; human-relations, at CUNA Mutual, 3, 109, 125, 126–27, 133, 135; participatory, 8–9; participatory, at CUNA Mutual, 117–20, 125, 137
"Management-by-objectives," 118
Managers: men as, 8, 18, 22, 23, 43–44, 49, 59; women as, 18, 33–34, 49–50
Manufacturers Hanover Trust Company, 9
Metropolitan Life Insurance Company, 9
Mills, C. Wright, 7

Index

National Labor Relations Board (NLRB), 49, 68, 80
National Staff Organization, 18
Negotiations. *See* Contract negotiations
Newsletters, workers', 123; at the Trust, 25, 27–28, 29–30, 31, 32, 54, 60
Nine to Five, 22
9 to 5: The National Association of Working Women, 1, 138

Office and Professional Employees International Union (OPEIU), 112
On the Front, 54
Open shop, 68, 73

Part-time workers, 76–79, 81, 137–38. *See also* Homeworkers, clerical
"Pin money," 21
Pooling arrangements, 10
Productivity standards. *See* Expectancies, productivity
Promotional opportunities: at CUNA Mutual, 116–18, 126; at the Trust, 19–20, 53; at WPS, 66
Prudential Insurance Company, 9

Quality circles, 8–9, 118–21, 125, 135, 137
Quitting, 3; at WPS, 3, 71, 82, 104–5, 132
Quotas, output. *See* expectancies, productivity

Recession of early 1980s, 53, 62, 81
REs (reasonable expectancies), 67, 68–70, 72–73, 79, 98, 102
Retail Clerks union (Local 1401), 66–67, 73–74

Salaries: at CUNA Mutual, 129; as factor in strike at the Trust, 33, 34; for homeworkers, 87, 90, 91, 93, 98, 101; at the Trust, 19, 26–27, 40–41, 55, 57; at WPS, 68, 81
Scientific management, 7, 8; at WPS, 68–70

Seafarth, Shaw, Fairweather, and Geraldson, 68, 84–85
"Secondary wage earners," view of women as, 6, 21, 23, 59, 101, 133, 134
Secretaries, 1, 116–17
Security Pacific National Bank, 9
Sexism, 8, 34, 43–44, 60, 136
Slowdown, 30
State Medical Society (SMS), 65
Strike at the Trust, 16; causes of, 16–17, 20–23, 33–34, 58–60; company's continued operation during, 34–35; demands of, 26–28, 33–34, 139; effects of, 17, 36–37, 49–54, 61–62; effects of, on workers' consciousness, 41–47, 57–58; meaning of, for understanding women's workplace activism, 58–62; outside support for, 39; picketing during, 34–36, 38, 39, 40; preparations for, 25–32; by management, 34–35; relation of workers' families to, 31, 36–37, 42; retaliation by management after, 47–49; settlement of, 40–41
Strikes, 131–32. *See also* Strike at the Trust; WPS, threatened strike at

Tardiness, 21
Taylorism, 82, 135
Teamsters Union, 78
Time and motion studies, 7, 68–69
Trust, the (Wisconsin Education Association Insurance Trust): automation at, 20, 50–53, 56, 61, 134–35; claims process at, 19, 20, 50–53, 56, 61, 134–35; claims process at, 19, 20, 50–53, 56, 61; class distinctions at, 21–22, 43, 56–57; contract negotiations at, 18, 21, 26–29; 31, 32, 53–55; contracts at, 21, 40, 52, 54–55; discrimination against women at, 28–29, 34, 43–44, 59–60, 136; geography of work at, 20–22, 24, 59, 130, 134; growth of, in 1970s, 18–19, 20; harassment of union activists at, 47–49; hierarchy at, 17–19, 22; promotional oppor-

Trust, the (*continued*)
tunities at, 19–20, 53; salaries at,
19, 26–27, 40–41, 55, 57; ties of, to
state teachers' union, 17, 39, 59, 65,
84, 130, 131; turnover at, 53, 62;
workers' newsletters at, 25, 27–28,
29–30, 31, 32, 54, 60; work rules at,
21–22, 27, 33, 40, 52, 54–56, 59–
60, 61. *See also* Strike at the Trust;
United Staff Union

Unions 5, 10–11, 45–47, 139, 140–
41; attitude of women clerical
workers toward, 24, 45–47. *See also*
AFL-CIO; CUNA Mutual, union at;
Local 1401; Local 1444; Strike at
the Trust; United Staff Union; WPS
unionization drive at
Union shop, 64, 74, 76
United Food and Commercial Workers (Local 1444), 74, 76, 77, 78–82,
103–4
United Professionals, 39, 44
United Staff Union (USU), 18, 24–25,
36, 47; women's partial autonomy
within, 25, 59, 130. *See also* Strike
at the Trust; Trust, the, harassment
of union activists at

Video-Display Terminals (VDTs), 50, 65

Wages. *See* Salaries
Wisconsin: progressive tradition in, 5;
unionization in, 5
Wisconsin Education Association
Council (WEAC), 17, 39, 49, 59
Wisconsin Education Association In-
surance Trust. *See* Trust, the
Wisconsin Physicians Services Insur-
ance Corporation. *See* WPS
Woman to Woman, 123
Women's Association, 3, 122–24, 131
Women's movement, 6, 44–45, 121, 134

Work rules: at the Trust, 21–22, 27,
33, 40, 52, 54–56, 59–60, 61; at
WPS, 68, 101
Work teams, 117, 135
"Work to rule," 48
WPS (Wisconsin Physicians Services
Insurance Corporation): anti-union
policies of, 67–68, 74, 103–4; anti-
union policies of, and hiring of
part-time workers, 76–79, 81, 86,
87–88; authoritarian policies of,
65–66, 70–71, 80, 82, 84, 115; automation at, 65, 73, 134–35; benefits
at, 66, 68, 81; lack of, benefits for
homeworkers, 87, 138; claims process at, 65, 67, 88–89; class distinctions at, 66–67; contract negotiations at, 68, 74–76, 80–81, 83; contracts at, 68, 74, 76, 79, 81, 87;
discrimination against women at,
74–75, 136; dress code at, 80, 85n6;
geography of work at, 64–65, 74,
83, 107, 130; growth of, 65, 74, 82,
87; harassment of union activists
at, 65, 67, 70–71, 74, 79–80; high
turnover at, 71, 73–74, 77, 83, 104–
5; part-time work at, 76–79; promotional opportunities at, 66; productivity standards ("reasonable
expectancies," or "REs") at, 67, 68–
70, 90, 98, 102, 135; resistance to
management policies at, 71–73;
salaries at, 68, 81; salaries for homeworkers, 87, 90, 91, 93, 98, 101; scientific management at, 68–70; successful intimidation of workers at,
71, 82, 83, 84, 104, 130–31, 132;
threatened strike at, 64, 75–76, 87;
union activism as response to authoritarian policies, 2–3, 79–80,
82, 130; unionization drive at, 2–3,
64–65, 67–68, 77–79, 82–83; workers' reactions to REs, 72–73; work
rules at, 68, 101

Note on the Author

Cynthia B. Costello received her Ph.D. in sociology from the University of Wisconsin in 1984 and spent a year at the Russell Sage Foundation as a postdoctoral fellow. She is the author of several articles on women's employment and collective action. She is currently the director of employment policy at Families USA Foundation in Washington, D.C.